HAZARDS

OF

ENTREPRENEURSHIP

A Guide to Business Success

by

Blossom O'Meally-Nelson, Ph.D

2000 Reprint

Published by
LMH Publishing Ltd.
P.O. Box 8296,
7 Norman Road,
LOJ Industrial Complex
Building 10
Kingston CSO, Jamaica
E-mail: lmhpublishing@cwjamaica.com

Cover Design: Errol Rhule
Typeset by Janet Campbell
Printed by: Lightning Print

ISBN 976-8184-03-5

Acknowledgements

To my two sons, entrepreneurs par excellence, and their wives;
To my daughter for her never-failing pragmatism;
To my mother for her tenacity in the face of every challenge;
To Billy Heaven for sharing his knowledge;
And to Marcia Higgens for her technical support.

A Joint Venture Project funded by The National Development Foundation of Jamaica (NDFJ).

Contents

Foreword

Dr. Blossom O'Meally-Nelson has written a very practical and readable book on the hazards of entrepreneurship.

It is particularly timely, given the protracted period of economic challenges experienced in this region over the last twenty years. Ideological shifts, changes in economic models, increasing layoffs, high unemployment and lack of social safety-nets have all combined to spur individuals to do something for themselves. More and more people are finding themselves in business, not from choice but because of the stark reality to survive. This is particularly true of our women who have traditionally shouldered the burdens of the breadwinner in developing countries such as ours.

Dr. Nelson is eminently qualified to write on the topic, having worked for many years in the National Development Foundation of Jamaica which has as its objective the development and support of the small business sector. As its Executive Director from 1987 to 1994 she saw at first hand the difficulties and concerns of the aspiring entrepreneur and I daresay she was moved to translate their difficulties and problems into positive guidelines for those who would follow in their paths.

She possesses an analytic, enquiring mind as well as an adventurous spirit; qualities which have led her from a career in teaching to one in business. I am sure she will forgive me if I say that in her venture into authorship she is already following the directions and advice outlined in the book.

I agree with her view that in Jamaica and the Caribbean there is no lack of entrepreneurial will. "What is needed... is a shaping of it, through the raising of consciousness and increasing the knowledge base so that the entrepreneur can know what skills are in his hands, he can know where opportunities exist and he can see himself as having some control over the way things will work out for him."

Entrepreneurship is both a science and an art and the book provides a practical approach written in an easy, lucid style. It discusses the significant factors affecting the start-up of the business and carries the entrepreneur through the A-Z of running the business and even looks into the challenge of the future.

This publication will prove a useful guide and prevent many from stumbling over unexpected obstacles. As one who began to tread this path some thirty years ago, I can empathise with the need for a publication such as this and would merely add, for the current generation of aspiring entrepreneurs, never let go of your dreams. Dare to follow your goals; dare to achieve; have faith in yourselves and seek to gain all the insight and knowledge that you can, along the way.

Hon. Danny Williams, OJ, CD, JP, CLU
President and Chief Executive Officer
Life of Jamaica Limited

Introduction

The word 'entrepreneur' which came into fashionable use in the eighties has now become the buzz-word of the nineties. Much generalised and often misused, this concept will form the central core of economic activity into the twenty-first century.

There are numerous studies and reports on entrepreneurial programmes and systems which operate mostly at the level of micro, small and medium scale enterprises. A large amount of development assistance has gone into funding credit programmes and in developing training packages and technical assistance interventions. These are designed to assist business operators and those contemplating setting up businesses to organise their endeavours in such a way as to gain maximum benefit from opportunities that exist and reduce the frustration that dogs every self-employed person.

The trend now is towards formalising entrepreneurial studies to the point where they may be regarded as a substantive science. The experience of India, for example, is one which has systematically given primacy to the development of entrepreneurship, entrepreneurial skills and entrepreneurial systems, and that country has many successes to show for its endeavours.

Entrepreneurial courses, separate and apart from business studies – although the basis for this separation may not be very clear – are now finding their way into universities and colleges. They are driven largely by the imperative to give students ready-to-use skills for the real world experience. Whether entrepreneurship can develop into an authentic science is another matter. One may well ask what purpose is to be served by more intensive study of this phenomenon as a separate body of knowledge. Would not an integrated approach suffice? It may well be that entrepreneurship is an art rather than a science, and may forever remain a hybrid construct hovering somewhere between human motivation and economic opportunity.

The word 'entrepreneur' was coined by a Frenchman, J.B. Say and came into use towards the end of the last century. It was intended to capture the concept of a type of 'creative destruction', a breaking down of old structures by the explosive energy of human initiative. The literal meaning indicates an activity which identifies the gaps in existing economic systems and sees them as opportunities rather than as deficiencies. The successful entrepreneur is the one who has the vision and the capability to capitalise on these gaps. Taken collectively, entrepreneurs can change the face of economic activity.

There are some societies which have identified a need for the promotion of entrepreneurship. This is in an effort to bring more players into a position where they can contribute to the gross domestic product. These strategies are intended to reshape thinking.

Global trends continue to indicate a pluralisation of economies as governments become impoverished and state enterprises are divested. Large conglomerates, too, face their challenges as they strain under their own weight, and display a slow absorptive capacity for the new technologies and a decreasing capability to respond to shifting market needs. Small businesses, on the other hand, driven by the entrepreneurial fervor to capitalise on the gaps created by these factors, have the flexibility which enables them to utilise technologies and systems to their advantage and to provide the service underpinnings for the giants which survive.

As the welfare state grows more bankrupt in ideas as well as in financial resources and is forced to abandon its role of sole provider for the many, individual endeavours will take centre stage, and the entrepreneurial approach will be further promoted and facilitated, particularly in Third World countries which have moved towards greater liberalisation of their economies.

In Jamaica, there is no lack of entrepreneurial will. Entrepreneurship has deep cultural roots which go as far back as Pre-Columbian times when Amerindian traders plied their accustomed routes, and exchanged trinkets, pottery and foodstuff through sophisticated barter systems with native Arawak Indians.

Slave societies had their Saturday markets and free men and

women engaged in providing a wide variety or services. Dressmakers, tailors, teachers, wheelwrights, blacksmiths, tinsmiths, boatmakers, other artisans and traders formed a vital part of the matrix which made Jamaica a viable colony.

The old city of Port Royal, before its destruction in the earthquake of 1692, housed intense commercial activity. The city was the most famous in the Western Hemisphere and formed the hub of activities, some of them illicit, as a gateway to the New World. The culture of independence and the desire for individual initiative bred in these early times persists.

A serious review then, of the role of entrepreneurship in this country's development would indicate that the entrepreneurial spirit has been alive and well for centuries. It is the driving force for endurance in the face of adversity. It is the creative energy which never says die. It is the will to begin again, over and over, because the sense of self is so strong and because life springs forward from the energy of our history and our latent creativity.

What is needed, therefore, in Jamaica and the Caribbean is not so much the promotion of entrepreneurship, as the shaping of it, through the raising of consciousness and increasing the knowledge base so that the entrepreneur can know the skills that are in his hands, he can know where opportunities exist, and he can see himself as having some control over the way things will work for him.

The most important feature of the entrepreneurial spirit is its creativity and its greatest asset its responsiveness. Entrepreneurial initiative springs from real needs and its expressions are as many and varied as the needs themselves. Thus, in Jamaica, informal commercial importers (or 'higglers') emerged as significant contributors to social stability in the late seventies and early eighties. Similarly, charcoal burners and distributors increased rapidly in number as oil prices increased and we now see the small business sector poised to take off in providing information processing services and in developing non-traditional exports as the imperatives for economic development change.

Very little has been written about entrepreneurship in economies in transition such as those of the countries of the

Caribbean Basin. What is presented here, is a simple, readable commentary which discusses the more significant factors affecting start-ups and business growth and the dynamics of the environment in which entrepreneurs operate.

This book, it is hoped, will give further inspiration to those brave – sometimes foolhardy – persons who believe it can be done, and will provide them with some useful tools for dealing with the problems that they face as well as providing information on sources of further assistance.

The Hazards of Entrepreneurship utilises a practical, conversational approach to the challenges and opportunities which exist in the world of business. It will provide useful tools for reassuring entrepreneurs that their experiences are not unique. It will help them to identify and categorise their problems, define the positive elements and move towards solutions.

HAZARDS

OF

ENTREPRENEURSHIP

A Guide to Business Success

1 Will the Real Entrepreneur Please Stand up?

The Entrepreneurial Debate

The question 'Who is an entrepreneur?' has been the subject of much discussion. Drucker, in his book *Innovation and Entrepreneurship* defines entrepreneurship as a style of management, he states:

> Management is the new technology (rather than the new science of invention) that is making the American economy an entrepreneurial one. It is also about to make America into an entrepreneurial society.

Drucker sees innovation as "the specific tool of entrepreneurs". For him the factor which drives entrepreneurship is changing technology, and entrepreneurship can be a structured response to the increasing economic dynamism of many societies. The seed of entrepreneurship lies in change and in the ability to see change as business opportunity. Drucker proposes that the time has come "to do for entrepreneurship and innovation what we first did for management in general" that is, "to develop the principles, the practice, and the discipline."

The more traditional definitions of entrepreneurship hold that the entrepreneur, by definition, shifts resources from areas of low productivity and yield to areas of higher productivity and yield and is seen to be a high risk activity. Drucker maintains that the entrepreneur is not necessarily engaged in high risk activity. For him, the risk occurs when entrepreneurs lack technology and management know-how. Very often, however, in the scheme of things, the entrepreneur creates resources through innovations of technology and finance rather than being the catalyst for what is merely a shift of resources from areas of low productivity to high productivity.

The concept of entrepreneurship, used here, is a more expansive one. To regard entrepreneurship as merely a response to newly emerging economic factors and technological advances, is to disregard the very nature of the concept and to deny it the essence of its validity. J.B. Say regarded entrepreneurship as evidence of dissent, a moving away from the normal response to prevailing economic systems. For him, the entrepreneur upsets and disorganises the status quo.

Joseph Schumpeter, a turn-of-the-century economist, perhaps came closest to mirroring what we are beginning to regard today as the characteristics of entrepreneurship. He saw entrepreneurship as independent of classic economic theory. For him it was an indefinable entity, (to be relegated perhaps to the realm of the paranormal). For Schumpeter the dynamic disequilibrium brought about by the entrepreneur is the symptom of a healthy economy rather than an indication of dysfunction.

It is perhaps the students of micro and small business development that have paid most attention to definitions and concepts, and who have sought most assiduously to make a case for entrepreneurship. E.F. Schumacher in his famous work *Small is Beautiful* sees as imperative, the 'humanization' of economic systems. He feels that the human race will not survive unless we achieve what is a sustainable lifestyle; in order to do this, individual needs must be the driving force of economic systems and the role of the individual must be identifiable.

The Quality of Entrepreneurship is not Strained...

The approach of the Government of India has been lauded as a suitable model for the promotion of entrepreneurship, particularly in Third World countries. The challenge of that country is to move from a predominantly traditional peasant society to one of innovation, industry and commerce, creating more contributors to the formal economy. Successive governments have had the task to "grow a nation" of business people.

It is little wonder then, that for that country entrepreneurship and entrepreneurial studies have become the central focus for what is, in fact, an economic revolution. Their approach is essentially an organic one, where entrepreneurship is considered in terms of the human responses to challenges. The behavioural aspects of entrepreneurship are emphasised. Self-confidence, risk-taking, planfulness and a range of psychological traits are seen as essential qualities for successful entrepreneurs. Businesses are nurtured, diagnosed when ill and "sicknesses" cured.

Any meaningful definition of entrepreneurship must take into consideration personality traits and must include creativity as a vital component. These must, however, be considered in the context of economic and political systems.

There is no doubt that economic hardship spawns entrepreneurs. The critical nature of economic depression and slow growth which impinges upon rich and poor alike sharpens the sensitivity to those gaps of opportunity which are created by the demise of some large businesses and the alternative technologies which must be utilised. Frequent lay-offs, difficulty in finding suitable jobs, low income, rising aspirations and expectations all serve to promote new business start-ups.

What really constitutes entrepreneurship? The soul of entrepreneurship resides in one's self-concept. How we see ourselves in relation to the world, our dreams, our aspirations, expectations and our beliefs about our ability to achieve and above all, our need to achieve.

Entrepreneurship is an approach, it is a way of seeing things and of doing things. Entrepreneurs can be found in the public sector as well as in the private sector, in business and in government; there is the entrepreneurial politician as well as the entrepreneurial neuro-surgeon. There are entrepreneurial managers, supervisors and workers.

The Entrepreneurial Awakening

For many, the first entrepreneurial stirrings came out of a dramatic life crisis, a dead-end work situation, injustice and lack of equity in the workplace or simply the belief that there must be something better.

For others it may be less dramatic: contracting public sector career opportunities, the economic instability to be found in developed and developing countries alike. The changing face of private enterprise with greater automation and new sophisticated technologies, threatens job security and forces once placid employees to think beyond the once safe havens of their companies.

The advent of the information superhighway has created possibilities for the individual that did not exist before. New types of service industries arise offering flexibility in location and requiring relatively little capital. All these serve to stimulate the entrepreneurial potential of persons seeking to increase their income and to test their capabilities.

Structural adjustment programmes, in countries such as Jamaica, have had a dramatically cathartic effect that has changed the social norms. Young men become higglers, traditionally women's work, and women take to the airways as traders, creating a whole new dynamic for dress, behaviour and family structure.

The reduction in public expenditure and drastic devaluation have made the income base for both rural and urban population inadequate. The pressure of population and diminishing land resources have given rise to a new breed of working class entrepreneur: in local parlance, "the hustler". Hustling, not in the sense used in North America, but rather as an approach to industry and to commercial activity, a will to make the best of opportunities, has seized the minds of working-class, middle-class and upper-class alike.

The economic uncertainties created by this rapid social change have made it necessary for individuals, particularly those at the bottom of the ladder to engage in new entrepreneurial initiatives. This is the spirit of entrepreneurship, the survival of the individual.

The Entrepreneurial Will

Entrepreneurial skills do not only serve for business start-ups. They are necessary in the day to day management of a business. Each day, for the business operator, brings new challenges related to production, financing, the management of human relations and service to the customer.

On a day-to-day basis the entrepreneurial qualities are tested and the entrepreneur is forced to examine his motives for being in business, evaluate his stance and strategise his response to hostile events or even to friendly approaches. Creativity, determination and insight as well as the will to bear the risk of the decision are the internal tools of the entrepreneur. Entrepreneurs, then, must see themselves as having the power to create change. They must be seized with the will to survive.

The strength of this will comes largely from the driving force or primary motivation which energises the entrepreneur. There are different types of entrepreneurial motivation.

The Reactive Entrepreneur

The reactive entrepreneur responds to some challenging situation such as job loss, inadequate income, obsolete or irrelevant skills, the death of a provider, divorce, unfavourable macro-economic trends. All these force the individual to produce a survival response, to create an independence and the capability to be flexible.

CASE IN POINT

Ruth in the Bible is perhaps, the most long-standing example of the reactive entrepreneur. Upon the death of her husband, she became a gleaner in the field of Boaz. Needless to say, her sales approach of providing ancillary services like that of washing Boaz's feet brought her the attention she deserved and assured her of her future fortune. Marion who has built a network of cottage craft producers for the export market is another example of the reactive entrepreneur. Her success was born of the need to survive after the death of her husband who was bread-winner.

The reactive entrepreneur seeks deep within the personal resources of determination and tenacity, coupled with technical aptitude and uses these to find suitable opportunities wherever they may be. "I have got to do something about this," is the key phrase that echoes in their thinking. Reactive entrepreneurs are usually structured and deliberate in their approach to their business ventures; their cause is not so much one of romance as of survival.

The Proactive Entrepreneur

The proactive entrepreneur is the one who has learnt early in the game that personal control over how one makes a living is the best means of ensuring economic survival. This is the go-getter and somewhat of a romantic, who is motivated largely by two things, the love of money and the will to capitalise upon opportunity. This person's creativity lies in the ability to see the opportunity and to shape the intervention to match this opportunity.

The proactive entrepreneur is likely to take more risks than the reactive entrepreneur. He is also likely to be involved in a greater number of ventures and to be more forward thinking in business concepts and technologies to be utilised.

CASE IN POINT

Martin, a successful radio talk-show host, who used his skill and wide audience to mobilise interest in business opportunities and then developed a range of financial services to serve his growing clientele is an example of a proactive entrepreneur. He had in fact created a new product – that of packaging radio in a user-friendly form and matching it with off-air services.

Entrepreneurship and Creativity

Innovation is often promoted as the hallmark of entrepreneurship. Yet, the innovator, the creator, the artist, the artisan, very often have few entrepreneurial skills. They tend to make their creation the central focus rather than the change that can be induced by that creation. The compulsion to protect the creation or innovative idea often blurs the vision to the opportunity, that gap in the economic fabric that will provide the springboard for their success.

Entrepreneurial creativity lies more in the ability to manipulate the existing situation to one's advantage, and to create the opportunities for the innovation than in the nature of the innovation itself. The entrepreneur must be able to see the relationships between events and systems and be able to predict trends or create them if need be.

Take for example, the number of products that have been

successfully marketed creatively utilising the Rastafarian mystique: from music, to hairstyles, to the use of colour and style of dress. An industry has been built on the Rastafarian philosophy and lifestyle. This industry is supported by the power of their ideas and the skill they bring to bear upon their craft: in short, their creativity.

Another Big 'E': Enthusiasm

There is one characteristic which is indispensable for the entrepreneur: it is enthusiasm. The entrepreneur must have a surplus of psychological and physical energy. There are no successful lazy entrepreneurs. There will be times, especially in the early years of a business venture, when survival depends upon sheer stamina, the energy to keep going one more hour to meet that deadline, and the will to try one more time. It is this energy which fires enthusiasm and enthusiasm can have an intoxicating effect; it can numb the pain of the many disappointments that are a part of the life of the entrepreneur. Thomas Fuller put it this way:

> The real difference between people is energy. A strong will, a settled purpose, and invincible determination, can accomplish almost anything: and in this lies the distinction between great people and little people.

A well-defined sense of self-determination and one's position in the scheme of things, a creativity which can be nurtured through practice and enlightenment must be underpinned by the will to take the risk. Risk-taking has been promoted as perhaps the most salient feature of entrepreneurship. It is not risk-taking per se that characterises the entrepreneur; he is not a mindless gambler, and this is not a game of chance. It is the risk one takes of relying upon one's own capabilities, of relying on the strength of an idea and the resilience that resides in flexibility.

Masochism or Entrepreneurship, is there a Difference?

Non-converts to the entrepreneurial philosophy tend to regard entrepreneurs with deep concern, and however much they may deny it, with some awe and more than a little envy. I grew up in a conservative family, where the emphasis was placed on academic achievement and professional qualification. Choosing a good solid profession and working hard at it was seen as the path to respectability and economic stability. The businessman or woman was regarded as the school drop-out, the non-achiever who had to choose a hard life fraught with risk, without the security of a government pension.

This was before the days of structural adjustment, high inflation, the stock market and tight monetary policy. It was also before the time when an entire generation of post-colonial professionals were subject to the bitter experience of the inadequacy of pensions. There is growing acceptance of operating a business as a respectable way of making a living for even the most educated of the middle and upper classes. Young MBAs today are anxious to wet their feet in the experience of business. This new fervour and strengthened confidence in the soundness of entrepreneurial endeavour, does not eliminate totally the feelings of apprehension among entrepreneurs.

Even where there is the firm decision to own and run a business, entrepreneurs often question themselves as to the wisdom of this, particularly when the going gets rough. "Why am I doing this to myself?" is the question often asked when interest rates on the bank overdraft soar and you had another unsuccessful day trying to clear goods from the wharf.

There is no doubt that masochism and entrepreneurship have a lot in common. For one, there is the wear and tear on the self. They both have this punitive element, where the individual goes headlong into events and situations which serve primarily to test his endurance. Participation in the annual trade fair is a good example of this. Long days of preparation, the expenses involved in putting together an attractive display, the dislocation of normal business operations, and long hours at the fair all add up to an exhausting experience. But, then, of course, you see it as a marketing opportunity.

Entrepreneurs and masochists tend to repeat time and time again the same negative experience. How many times did you lose a shipment of goods, without putting proper insurance in place? How many times did you manufacture too many of the odd colour shirts? And how many times did you fail to make your financial returns in time to avoid penalties?

Like the masochist, the entrepreneur finds pleasure in the pain, or perhaps, if not pleasure, at least a sense of worth – the type of feeling that can be supported by the well-known lines, "The glory lies in the struggle, not the prize." Perhaps this is not a bad thing. After all, such values have formed the cornerstone of the British educational system. The bad thing is, however, that it need not to be so, at least not all of the time.

The Pseudo-Entrepreneur

Times of rapid technological change and unsettled economic systems, tend to breed a type of pseudo-entrepreneurial restlessness, where business start-ups become the fashion, and to own a business is seen as a status symbol. In Jamaica it is called 'trying a ting,' and the 'trying man' has become the symbol of the oppressed and of social change. The term pseudo-entrepreneurial is used here, because the symptoms mimic those of the real entrepreneur. But they lack depth, and are in fact an adopted stance, a fashion, a type of mass hysterical response to the current thinking. Pseudo-entrepreneurs lack the staying power of their more soundly-rooted counterpart.

Needless to say, the pseudo-entrepreneur is more prone to the hazards of entrepreneurship, where business ventures chosen might not match personal skills and competences, and where the basic motive is not rooted in a deep desire to succeed in this chosen path but, rather, like the proverbial seed that fell on stony ground, they spring up but are soon withered by the sun of hardship. These account for the major part of the statistics for business failure.

The Real Entrepreneur

The real entrepreneur, then, is the one who brings to the endeavour whatever it may be – whether in government, commerce, manufacture, agriculture, the professions – the eagle eye for opportunity, the ability to perceive new possibilities for systems and processes and the motivation to create change. The entrepreneur is willing to operate in the realm of the unknown, to explore the uncharted perimeters of possibility, and like the eagle, to live by that unerring internal map.

Finally, the entrepreneur must be an activist. Without implementation, entrepreneurial ideas remain pipe dreams and wasted opportunities. The real entrepreneur engages the day-to-day world in a creative and productive struggle.

2 WOMEN AS ENTREPRENEURS

Without Being Sexist

One must always think carefully before introducing gender into any discussion. Whatever approach is used, chances are someone will be offended. My own philosophy tends to regard gender differences as being more the result of socialization and societal expectations rather than upon genetic programming.

Do Women Work?

There has been much research and discussion centred around the topic of women and work.

For many husbands, it is more acceptable for wives to be self-employed than to seek employment. There is less threat to the man's capability to care for his family than if the wife holds a highly paid job. One suspects that in this circumstance it is easier to pass off the wife's efforts at developing a business as something more of a whim than as of serious concern.

In North America the growing number of female entrepreneurs is well documented. Women are starting new businesses twice as fast as men in the USA; in Canada, they own one-third of the small businesses. In France, one-fifth of small businesses is woman-owned. In Britain, for the decade of the eighties, the number of self-employed women increased three times as fast as that of men. In Jamaica women own approximately 40% of small businesses. Women as consumers, producers of wealth, and movers of capital are well on their way to being the economic force of the future.

It is ironic that women in developing countries have a longer and more intimate relationship with entrepreneurship than their North American counterparts. In Caribbean slave societies it was the women who traded ground provisions and exchanged goods in the Saturday markets. It is the women who today account for the majority of higglers or traders. Their sales have extended from ground provisions to a multiplicity of items, and markets now extend beyond national boundaries. This form of trading has proven to be the main source of income for working-class families particularly in developing countries. In Jamaica, many men have now followed suit and have adopted this form of livelihood.

The convenience of operating a small business from home offers relief from a lifetime of frustration with the domestic role and opens the opportunity to generate an income to meet real family needs. Self-owned enterprises also allow women to avoid the negative factors which may operate against them in the workplace.

Many women, having secured a place in the world of work, face the reality of gender bias in promotion practices which reduces their chances of upward mobility despite their obvious competence. Their penchant for entrepreneurship, in this case, may be based more on necessity than on raw entrepreneurial verve.

Family Considerations

A woman usually enters the world of entrepreneurship with some constraints; she finds that she will have to operate within the context of family with minimal cash resources, and generally less support from family and friends than her male counterpart. Very often she is not taken seriously in the initial stages of her endeavour, but may nevertheless be indulged by those who care about her.

The situation of Blondie and Dagwood, comic strip characters, presents an interesting scenario. Blondie has recently turned entrepreneur, setting up a catering business and receiving support from an initially bewildered Dagwood, who eventually becomes far too enthusiastic when he sees the opportunities for indulging in his favourite pastime – eating!

For women, the hazards of entrepreneurship based upon family considerations are more crippling than for men. Women have been known to virtually abandon their businesses when the significant men in their lives decide to engage in not-so-subtle psychological warfare.

Men are particularly prone to feelings of loss of control when their spouses begin the journey into entrepreneurial obsession. This may manifest itself in unsupportive behaviour, making the woman's life as an entrepreneur even more difficult.

The will to overcome these initial hurdles has to be strong for women, even moreso than for men. Life as an entrepreneur has greater implications for a woman's self-identity and in defining her goal. If she is within a marriage she has to consider the reaction of her husband and children to this change in lifestyle. She will have less time for them, and her newly found activities will impinge upon their lifestyle. Some degree of consensus about her new enterprises is therefore necessary.

If her husband is an employee rather than a businessman in his own right, his wife's penchant for risk-taking, her determination to seek gratification from her endeavours, as well as the possibility of significant growth in her income, are factors that will colour his perception of her and their relationship. This may require a reinterpretation of the way they communicate and relate to each other. There is clearly now a different agenda and a new dimension to her life.

For a woman, a successful business means economic independence. This has serious implications for the stability of her relationship with her spouse, especially if he has always seen himself as the bread-winner. Some women seek to mitigate this risk by down-playing the success of their businesses, by pretending or continuing to be dependent on the spouse for simple decisions – "We will see what George has to say" – or to generally seek to include the spouse in the business by assigning him some worthwhile task.

Pregnancy, etc....

Studies have shown that the most prevalent factors affecting the performance of women-owned businesses are the social factors which have to do with health and family commitments. An unplanned pregnancy, in the case of a sole proprietor, can be fatal to the business. The woman finds that, of necessity, she has to be out of the business for some months and remains somewhat distracted for the next two years at least. This is particularly critical in the case of a single mother. For a woman, then, a supportive spouse and the presence of the extended family can enhance her chances of success.

Whenever there is illness in the family, an ageing parent to care for, or some family crisis, it is usually the woman who is called upon to fulfill the role of nurse, housekeeper, driver, banker, handyman, and to perform a host of other services which may be needed from time to time. In all of this, she will not be able to give the necessary time and attention to her business, and may, in fact, have to cease operating.

Women and their families need to plan for these contingencies in advance. There should be some commitment to shifting roles and tasks, and responsibilities should be shared in a more equitable manner.

Working-class women generally have fewer alternatives than their middle-class sisters. Their families so desperately need the additional income that considerations of power and the more delicate nuances of intimacy are overshadowed by the practicality of what has to be done. This is not to say that in these households problems related to the woman's involvement in business and her earning power do not arise. They tend, however, not to occupy a central place because of the more basic needs to be filled by the additional income. In fact, often there is resentment on the woman's part when the business succeeds, that she is the main bread-winner, yet she is still expected to continue the 'female' role.

The good news is that there are many sound marriages in which the wife is a successful businesswoman and earns the respect and support of her husband and children. There are also strong husband and wife teams where the wife may give up a lucrative job to join her husband in the business. It all depends upon the personalities involved, the business' scope for supporting both partners, the strength of the relationship and the nature of the hidden agendas which are being played out in their day-to-day world of business.

A woman must develop the ability to give primacy to the needs of her business in the hope that genuine love and unselfishness will prevail.

Take a Giant Step

If a woman is single, she will have more freedom to choose the type of business venture she would like to engage in, but then will generally have less support systems in place for realising her dream, particularly where the extended family is absent, when she may find herself truly on her own. She also has to consider what would be the implications for her life as a businesswoman if she were to get married. Would she have to close shop in order to take on her new role as wife and mother? There are still unmarried women who are hesitant to appear financially independent because they feel that this lessens their chances of finding a husband – as if a husband were some commodity incompatible with entrepreneurial endeavours.

A woman's decision to take up the entrepreneurial flag or not will be based on her self-concept, whether or not she sees herself as a competent adult, capable of defining her own life preferences. Her self-concept is the springboard for other entrepreneurial characteristics such as the ability to plan, the strength of her motivation, tolerance of risk and a generally positive view of life.

A woman's self-concept is based on a complex of factors starting from the intra-uterine environment before birth. The experiences of bonding with the mother figure, the communication with the father figure, and the sibling environment, all lead to the development of interpersonal trust and confidence in one's own abilities.

In situations where the child is constantly denigrated and made to feel inferior, chances are that a negative concept of self will develop which will be difficult to overcome in adult years. Children who have consistently positive experiences as they learn new skills, and who grow up in an environment where they can be open and trusting have a greater sense of personal efficacy and a more positive self-concept.

One of the greatest hurdles to overcome is the deep sense of guilt that plagues women, whether consciously, or unconsciously when they do not opt to give primacy to child-bearing and family. The constant effort to swim against the tide of social convention can be quite enervating, but she must bear in mind that with any luck she can have the best of both worlds.

For many a woman the process of deciding to follow her entrepreneurial urge is a long and painful one, where the fear of failure looms large and threatens to engulf the small flame of business opportunity. There comes a time, however, when she may be possessed of a desperate sense to take control of her own life and save herself, to establish her individuality rather than face oblivion. She may reach that point of frustration that is expressed by Sarah Rath:

> I have served my quiet term of desperation:
> Diapers and dishpans,
> egg salad sandwiches for the social.
> ...I have been to eighty and
> back again
> these nine years.

Following The Dream

Having established the strength of the social and psychological parameters within which she will operate, the woman must now turn to the matter of interest. She must determine what consumes her interest, what area of the world of enterprise fills her with fascination and fires the motivational drive. She may say that she doesn't care very much what she does, so long as she makes money. Well, be that as it may, other women, however, are more likely to see their enterprise as an extension of themselves, as a channel for self gratification and self actualisation.

Michael Gerber maintains that "your business is not your life." Tell that to a woman! He advocates working *on* your business, not *in* it. But so fierce is the possessiveness of a woman towards her business that she serves it rather than have it serve her. It is that intimate linkage that fuels the tenacity with which women approach enterprise, with a will to ride out every storm and reach safe harbour. It is this same tenacity, however, which makes it so difficult to advise her as to what course of action to take, as blind determination eclipses full-sighted reason.

The area of interest chosen is best supported by some form of aptitude. This talent need not only manifest itself in technical skills, although these may form a good basis for her entrepreneurial endeavour. Culinary arts, dress-designing, pattern-making, craft and the aesthetic fields all offer unbounded opportunities.

More importantly, aptitude also resides in the intellectual skills which guide the fast-growing areas of service industries: marketing, software packaging, printing, health care and management services. Statistics show that, as women on the whole achieve a higher educational level than men, the rise of knowledge-industries and the dawning of the information age create a business environment which will be to their benefit.

A woman need not be guided by old stereotypes; she can break into new unconventional areas of business, provided that she is prepared to negotiate, with courage and determination, the hazards which present themselves. She should not see herself as disadvantaged because of her sex, but rather as empowered. Let's not forget that in the natural scheme of things women have been forced to develop coping skills and to look deep within themselves for answers. Ashly Montagu writes of the so-called 'woman's intuition':

> Women have to keep their eye on the main chance, they have to be on their guard; they must always have their antennae extended, without appearing to do so, so that they may operate on the correct wave-length and pick up the proper signals without anyone noticing, as it were.

A woman, then, is theoretically more prepared for surviving the hazards of entrepreneurship than a man. Her greatest enemy is herself. How she reacts to the perennial temptation to lapse into old stereotypic modes and lose control of the dominant role of entrepreneur, making it subservient to her roles of wife, of entrepreneur, making it subservient to her roles of wife, mother, daughter or lover, will determine her success in the world of business.

...And the Obstacles

Lack of access to credit has been touted as one of the primary hindrances to women going into business. Certainly, in many traditional societies where women are held in submission and are not generally counted as contributors to Gross Domestic Product the task of revolutionising the economic systems to the extent that women can gain access to formal credit is an arduous one, and one to which increasing attention is being given through numerous credit programmes and initiatives to improve women's legal status.

The United Nation's Charter on Women holds as important the economic advancement of women through their integration into formal economies worldwide. There is the widely held view that if women are targeted to receive the financial resources to enable them to increase their earning power, this will have a far greater effect in alleviating poverty among disadvantaged groups, than if the resources are made available only to men, since women show a greater resourcefulness and commitment to family.

In the Caribbean, barriers to credit for women are more attitudinal than structural. Except where credit programmes are specially designed with flexible collateral requirements, and these are mainly for poverty alleviation rather than economic growth, women are forced to face the stringent scrutiny of bankers who, however sympathetic they might be, have a duty to protect their depositors' money. They need to be assured that women are serious about remaining in business in the long term and that adequate collateral can be provided.

Traditionally, women have not been the holders of property, neither have they accumulated appreciable amounts of capital – the focus being on sons receiving inheritance rather than daughters. Bankers, somehow, have respect for the marriage union and for the laws which govern rights to property. They are careful, therefore, to secure the husband's consent when making loans to a married woman. And, in fact, in some countries, where the husband is liable for all debts incurred by his wife, this is a *legal* requirement. This situation is likely to remain until women find means of accumulating their own capital, whether individually or in consortia and of acquiring property and the type of fixed assets which can be used to secure debt equity, and to change the laws.

The following summarises the impediments to women as entrepreneurs:

- fear of failure: the difficulty in making that quantum leap into the world of entrepreneurship;
- family considerations: the attitude of the spouse and the requirements of child-rearing or care-giving where parents are involved;
- lack of capital: failure to form a capital base and to attract debt equity;
- inability to separate personal, emotional and social needs from the needs of the business;
- failure to inspire confidence of banks and support agencies;
- inability to focus on business problems and develop solutions;
- tendency to seek approval rather than make independent decisions on a timely basis;
- lack of confidence in their own capabilities;
- failure to manage health;
- succumbing to stress rather than prioritising activities and taking control.

Each one of these impediments is manageable, through personal development programmes which create greater self-awareness and emotional independence, and through informed financial engineering which will utilise creative means of securing the equity needed for mobilisation of entrepreneurial activity.

Tomorrow's woman must begin today, to prepare herself for her new role as frontrunner in business.

3 WHERE DO YOU GO FROM HERE?

The Entrepreneurial Bug

All but the most complacent are seized from time to time with the entrepreneurial fever. When the bug bites and the infection sets in, it is best to recognise it for what it is worth. At its simplest it is an implosion of will that eventually possesses the mind and sharpens one's awareness of the possibilities that exist. It motivates the type of introspection that serves to clarify one's aspirations and expectations.

There is no telling what might trigger this entrepreneurial fever. It may be an unexpected encounter with a schoolmate who opted for the unconventional and the risky, that restless exhibitionist who always dreamt a little harder than the rest, and had little time for the present trials of schooling but who instead had that characteristic tunnel vision that marks those who look much to the future.

"Who would believe that John Brown who used to collect old cricket balls and sell them would have actually hit the big times?" you ask. Upon this encounter, you too realise that in fact, life is passing you by, that the very things which you were taught to value – conformity, the respect for social norms, the willingness to bear responsibility, to be cooperative and supportive and to be in fact a "good citizen" – are the very things that are now weighing you down into mediocrity and ultimate underachievement.

This is not to say that successful entrepreneurship presupposes irresponsible behaviour. The entrepreneurial spirit does not promote socially dysfunctional persons as its ideal. It does, however, state that inner desire to change things for the better and to test your potential. In short, the 'winter of your discontent' is in fact the rustling of your latent entrepreneurial energy which can point you to new horizons and undreamed of achievements.

Or, your trigger may be that you are one of those who have suffered some life trauma: the death of a spouse or parent who was chief breadwinner, divorce, the loss of property, disability, or the need to leave your accustomed surroundings for a new location. Whatever may be your circumstance, and it may be a combination of some of the above, the entrepreneurial energy beckons you to action.

If your trauma has been severe, depression and mental confusion cause a lack of the confidence needed to fire the entrepreneurial will. You are left exhausted and overwhelmed by the magnitude of what is to be done. Even the matter of filling out an application form for a bank loan becomes an imposition too hard to bear.

If you find yourself in such a position it is important for you to develop, first of all, the capability to be objective. You have to, in reality, become a participant-observer in your own life and to create what some psychologists call that "supra-self" which is able to define and analyse your feelings and motives and to separate that part of you which guides you rational thinking – the survival instinct.

The supra-self then, is that part of your consciousness that remains capable of reasoning with some clarity, that employs logical thinking and develops the coping mechanisms for the periodic onslaughts of the depressed, traumatized, or grieving self. It is the part of you that causes you to say, like Mia Farrow, "I can't go on, I can't go on, I can't go on, so I guess I had better get up and go on."

Having pin-pointed the existence of the survival instinct, for many it is equivalent to the faint trace of a pulse in the dying man which the medics use to justify the kiss of life. For others it is stronger, more resolute and determined, it is already burning. Whatever may be the state of your survival instinct you must nurture it by focusing on it and giving it the time and the energy necessary to spawn itself. Like the mushroom in the dark, it can take on unprecedented dimensions and in time will take primacy over disabling psychological responses.

Choosing Your Business

You are now ready to consider some new endeavour. You have cleared your vision, you are now able to see the entrepreneurial opportunities and to see how they match your interests and aptitudes. This is the place where you determine the goods or service which you must offer.

In order to do this you must first think carefully about your attitude to people. There is no insulation of the entrepreneur from people. People in the entrepreneur's life occur singly or in group. Family, employees, creditors, suppliers, competitors, customers are all to be part of the matrix of relationships and must each be treated in the appropriate style.

Ted S. Frost, in his highly readable work, *The Second Coming of the Woolly Mammoth* writes an open letter to would-be entrepreneurs in which he states:

> The reasons people skills are so important is that business is not an abstract activity. The business world is a living, breathing thing composed of interaction between human beings. It is the interactions that are key. There are many people walking around with technical capability and intelligence and good ideas, but the ones most likely to succeed financially are those adept at dealing with others, those who can sell themselves to others and get people to like them.

In choosing your business then, you must consider the type of people that you will have to deal with and resolve to develop the necessary interpersonal skills to do so. You will no longer have the luxury of intolerance for even the most obvious pipsqueak who may dog you.

If you are a professional, your choice of form of business is equally challenging. The time was, when the success of the doctor, the lawyer, the dentist, the teacher was a given. One was guaranteed an adequate income and could even hope for wealth. Certification, integrity, reasonable professional competence and a suitable site for one's shingle were what it took for success.

Today, with increased access to education and the resulting mobility across class structure, traditionally elitist professions are becoming more commonplace. Advances in technology and a more knowledgeable society are forcing professionals to think of the customer and the market, to seek alternative sources of income; and in short to behave like entrepreneurs.

You may be such a professional who must decide whether to leave institutional employment, a partnership or consortium, or whether in fact, to strengthen the partnership or consortium.

The Importance of the Mustard Seed

CASE IN POINT

Carmen was a young attorney-at-law who worked first in a law firm, gaining considerable experience in conveyancing. The major partners, all older men, with the settled lifestyle of the legal elite were conformist and stodgy and showed no propensity to move with the times.

After three years of drudgery, Carmen decided that it was time to move on. This time she secured a position in a financial institution and took charge of the legal department. The processing of loan documents was fairly routine, but the legal aspects of loan recovery strategies provided some exciting moments.

After gaining further skills in drafting agreement and financial instruments Carmen was bitten by the entrepreneurial bug. The yearning to be her own boss, to determine her own income and to choose the types of cases she would prefer became more and more compulsive.

Eventually, Carmen decided to hang out her own shingle. Enter fear of the unknown. The field of law was becoming increasingly competitive as more and more graduates moved into the arena. Continued high inflation meant that the overhead costs for setting up business were high. Image required that she had a suitable office, but office space was scarce and where available expensive. For her to attract clients, who would more likely be her age peers she needed high tech equipment. The computer and fax machine were a necessity, and a typist/receptionist had to be hired. She also faced one significant other expense. Having driven a company car for her working life, she would now have to purchase her own.

Despite her sound entrepreneurial intentions, Carmen was faced with concrete realities about which decisions had to be made. Should she sacrifice image in the short term and be downbeat in her selection of office space, or even share an office with a colleague in the first instance and use common services? The choice here depended on the level of equity available as well suitable possibilities for loans.

Carmen, in the five years since her graduation, had managed to generate enough equity through savings and investments to provide some collateral for a loan to purchase the equipment and furnishings necessary. She has also, during this time, done much private work for a growing clientele. She knew that in order to retain their confidence her new business must have the appropriate image and capacity.

Carmen found that it was one thing to access the capital needed for business start-up and it was another to generate the cash flow necessary for servicing the debt and feeding herself. She now recognised that the matters of sales and collections were no different for her than for the clients on whose behalf she sought to recover debt. What guarantee did she have that she would receive business on a continuous basis, let alone get paid for it? Here she recognised that she needed to utilise that most indispensable of all the entrepreneurial skills, faith. **You will not reach very far in your business venture without faith.**

This faith is driven by a positive view of life. A belief that in the world of endeavour your product is comparable and even better that others. You believe in your ability to influence others and to attract them into the circle of your effort. You believe that you can build a clientele because of who you are and the competence which you bring to bear on the conduct of your business. You have faith in the competitive edge which you must create.

CASE IN POINT

Beverley had spent the last ten years as chief "girl" in a hair-dressing parlour. Her skills and competence and warm personality enabled her to attract and retain a fairly large clientele. The fact that she was willing to train and supervise the other girls meant that she was the mainstay of the business. Her employer was unwilling to offer her shares in the ownership and Beverly saw herself continuing for years with a level of wages that would never allow her any significant accumulation of capital.

She sought advice from a financial agency engaged in the field of business development. She wanted to set up her own business. She

> asked herself, "Why can't I do it for myself, must I give my skill and energy always to make someone else rich?" This is the crossroads for many would-be entrepreneurs – when they recognise that the high returns in the business are due mainly to their efforts, and that their wage levels are not a just compensation for their efforts. They have played no mean part in the generation of profits, without adequate reward or significant future gain. At this point it is time to think seriously about setting up your own business.

The argument used by most employers in a case such as this is that they are taking the risk, they had to bear start-up costs, hedge against inflation and bad times, and face replacement costs for equipment in the future. These very factors will prove the greatest deterrent to Beverly as she considers going on her own. Hairdressing and cosmetology are capital intensive activities. The specialised equipment needed is expensive. Products which come in an almost infinite variety are costly, pricing of services must be competitive, and in order to increase productivity one must increase the amount of equipment and employees, which in turn sends up costs.

Beverley, if she wishes to fulfill her entrepreneurial dreams with her minimal resources, will have to move to a less expensive location, forego the use of state of the art equipment, reduce the variety of products which she offers and hope that under these circumstances she can retain her old clientele. She has, of course, another option, which is one often pursued by the new entrepreneur. She can seek equity investments from people who have the money but no skills and negotiate to exchange her skills for equity. She would then be part owner with the option to increase her shares as the business grows.

What you face then, is a two-pronged dilemma: how to garner the resources to make this critical initiative, and how to sustain it once you have made it. This is an age-old dilemma. The Children of Israel faced it as they prepared to leave Egypt and peered apprehensively into the desert. Many an entrepreneur has no Moses to blame and is left, often hounded, by a concerned family to wonder whether it would not have been better indeed to be satisfied with their former status, however lowly.

CASE IN POINT

In my own case, my personal dilemma was no less daunting. Having spent sixteen years as an educator and having achieved the highest qualifications in the field I faced a cross-roads. It seemed as if everything converged upon that place. Professional burn-out, the collapse of a marriage, the beginning of mid-life and the shadow of the empty nest. In Jamaica, there is a proverb where the folk-hero Anancy wisely declares that "two troubles are better than one." I had them all.

I had long felt the ennui, the discontent, the restlessness, which although I did not know it then, was the stirring of the entrepreneurial spirit, that feeling that there must be something better. I had found it hard to conceptualise going into my own business. The fact was, that my skills were not largely transferable, so I sought job after job, with little success. The reasons? I was over-specialised and over-qualified. I have often said that I owe my success to the people who wouldn't hire me.

My first venture into entrepreneurial activity was to sell the idea to a Management Institute to allow me to set up operations for them in another town. I managed to get them to catch the vision and in no time embarked upon my project which was a resounding success. The spin-off for me was that I got management training free of cost. I had begun my much needed re-tooling.

From then on, there was no turning back. I had found the nexus, the bridge across which I would transfer my skills of communication, analysis and evaluation, gleaned from years of experience as an educator to forge for myself a new rewarding professional life. Yes, there were many days when I couldn't pay my bills, but in time, those days got further and further apart.

The decision to take that fateful step from steady employment, whatever its conditions, is never an easy one. It is the decision which faces the newly feathered chick secure in his nest, except of course if his mother makes it for him! It is the decision which faces the baby standing firm on his own two feet at last, but how to let go, let alone make the first step? It is only that faith, confidence, enthusiasm and need to create and explore which drives both bird and child. It is unthinkable that either would decide against taking that fateful step, think of what would be lost to them! In the same way you will realise that there is too much to be lost in experience and self-fulfillment not to try.

Making the Best of Your Skills

There are those of you, however, who were not born entrepreneurs, neither did you choose entrepreneurship. You, in fact, had entrepreneurship thrust upon you. You have no alternative! Job loss, redundancy, economic downturn, all serve to contract the job market and to trigger the survival instinct. You must seek alternatives to employment, you must start your own business.

As Moses stood in the wilderness, at a loss as to what to do, he was engaged in what was perhaps one of the greatest entrepreneurial adventures of all times, he certainly had a troublesome and easily dissatisfied clientele! God said to him, "What is in thy hand?" Now, as far as Moses was concerned, this was the same old weatherworn stick that he had used to aid his surefootedness for many years. It was not particularly significant, at least not until he used it to strike the rock and opened up a whole new dimension of miraculous possibility.

The situation is no different with many of us. We have taken our skills for granted, and we have devalued our well-worn tools, the things that have the potential to create for us our own miracles. Your first task therefore is to take stock of what is in your hand. What skill do you have? What experience? How adaptable are you? How open to new ideas?

CASE IN POINT

For the Stokes brothers, it was the new and the unforeseen: the idea that a bob-sleigh team from a tropical country could compete in the Winter Olympics. Their physical prowess and intellectual daring provided the fuel for the entrepreneurial fire, as they, along with the other members of that history-making team, with scarce resources and second-rate equipment showed the determination to compete with and beat some of the best teams.

It was not so much the gap in performance that presented the greatest challenge, it was the financial gap, the lack of funds necessary to make their dream a reality. The ability of that first group of managers and team members to raise money is now legendary.

For some people it is a hobby which they have enjoyed over the years. Making dried floral arrangements for example, bottled pickles, yogurt, decorative baskets, dolls or monogrammed bed linen; your hobby may be marketable. The world of business is replete with the success stories of people who have made their hobbies into income-generating businesses.

CASE IN POINT

Jennifer Samuda of Jencare Skin Farm, has had a life long interest in cosmetics and good skin. At high school she excelled in the sciences but did not have the resources to pursue a degree in bio-chemistry. She had to take up work in a bank. Jennifer never gave up on her dream, however. She started experimenting in her spare time with various cosmetics and offered facials to her friends. Soon she began to develop her own products and techniques. She was an avid reader and kept abreast of the latest research and trends in the management of ageing and general skin health.

Jennifer recognised that the timing and pacing of her business was of the greatest importance, her products had to be tested, licensed and sold in sufficient quantities to support the cost of manufacture. Pricing was of significant importance to her as she had a commitment to the mass market, in spite of the fact that what she was producing were in fact exclusive products that could successfully service the upper end of the market and take their place beside Elizabeth Arden, Germaine Monteil and Lancôme.

The greatest challenge to Jencare Skin Farm was to secure adequate foreign currency to purchase raw materials for manufacture. This led to Jennifer's decision to set-up operations in Miami through a consortial arrangement with a dermatologist. You will recognise that here, the entrepreneurial energy came to the fore. Married, and a mother of two, with a full-time job and with the burning passion to grow her business, what Jennifer has done is as much a feat of physical energy as it is of intellectual competence and psychological stability.

Jennifer is the proactive entrepreneur par excellence. Today she is full-time into her business. It has expanded into a number of countries and her products have won international acclaim. Yet she still finds time to give individual attention to her customers. She likes people!

Whose Preference, Yours or Your Customer's?

There are, unfortunately, instances where the would-be entrepreneur's love of a product becomes an obsession. This usually happens to those engaged in the production of some craft item.

Take for example the young woman, who having achieved some competence in ceramics manufacture decided to go into business of her own. Her favourite items were reproductions of animals: dogs, cats, roosters, hens which were painted in gaudy colours. What she failed to recognise was that her personal preference in colour was not acceptable to her customers, that the wider, more sophisticated market demanded ceramics of a different size and colour range. She did not have the luxury of the artist to believe in her own work, she had to consider demand and preference.

This is not to say that there is no room to shape consumer preference. The famous story of the company which made millions of dollars through the sale of pet rocks is a memorable example of the power of marketing that capitalises on fads and fashions. This unique idea addressed specifically the human need to nurture and appealed to a market which could not express this need because of the stressful demands of urban living.

The teddy bear, Gund toys, Barbie Bolls all appeal to the need to nurture and to belong. Attendant upon this is the human compulsion to collect. This is the source of mounting sales in doll collections, porcelain items, curios, statuettes, books and a range of possibilities. It only takes some thinking on the part of the artisan to have the market anxiously waiting for the next piece.

You may not be the artistic type. You have determined that the headache of manufacture and marketing is beyond you, you prefer the service industry. There are services which require specific skills and those which do not. Personal and health care services, for example, require trained personnel, but can attract a lucrative market.

You should take time out to determine whether your skill is on the brink of obsolescence. Take, for example, printing. It seems that there is a printer in everyone dying to get out. The truth is that the printing press is heading for obsolescence and new computer technology has taken over, offering by far a wider range of possibilities in a shorter time. Today we can be our own printers.

Straight commercial activity, such as trading, can be entered into by virtually anyone, provided that you are prepared to acquire the necessary business skills. The challenge here is to find your market niche, that location and set of people who need to purchase the products you are opting to sell. Your choice of specialisation is also important. The general economic environment must indicate to you that there will be a demand for the range of items that you offer.

Personal Considerations

There are certain factors, which though they may appear intangible at the outset, nevertheless hold serious implications for your success as an entrepreneur. The personal hazards which you may face could prove to be the most crippling. What of your health? Are you prone to long periods of illness? There are those, who for example, suffer greatly when exposed to certain chemicals which activate allergies and other reactions. Back problems, varicose veins and female disorders are other culprits. Lost work time due to illness can play havoc with your business. If you are likely to be ill for significant periods, then you must plan for this and seek to put the appropriate management in place so that the business can continue during your periods of illness.

There are in fact, those who are forced to choose a line of business which is compatible with their disability. Take the young micro-business operator for example who could no longer tolerate the glare from his welding equipment. After two bouts of eye surgery he was forced to re-tool and develop skills in machinery repair instead.

It is always a challenge to recognise when it is not in your best interest to seek to continue in a particular line of business for health reasons, and it takes courage to re-tool and redirect your efforts. Letting go can be just as difficult as letting go a lost love, so deep is the true entrepreneur's attachment to his chosen occupation.

Then there is the matter of family. This is particularly critical for those who are planning to leave their jobs, which, however unsatisfactory, at least provided a paycheck. To venture into the uncharted waters of new entrepreneurial endeavour is another matter. One thing is certain, your new business will have a profound effect on your home life, things will change, for better or for worse.

Your first selling job, then will be to your spouse. A sympathetic and supportive wife or husband is an unusual benefit to be treasured. New business activity undoubtedly puts a strain on a marriage, or other forms of co-habiting or conducting relationships (there are so many alternatives these days!).

Firstly, it may be recognised that the entrepreneur is in love with his or her idea, that this love, in order to bear fruit must be as obsessive as any other love. The love object requires attention. It consumes the mind and requires your physical presence, often at odd hours. It makes you tired physically, emotionally and intellectually. Is there room in your life for more than one love object? A sympathetic spouse who can catch the vision, who actually believes in you and your idea, who can stand in the background while you nurture your new found love, can be a tower of strength to you. Provided, of course that you do not abuse this understanding and you do have the discipline to make time for him or her.

Secondly, it must be recognised that disruptions in the normal scheme of things are inevitable. The living room may suddenly be full of boxes, and one bedroom sacrificed as a storage area. The kitchen becomes a workshop and the telephone is no longer accessible. It is more often attached to an answering machine in case the customer calls and no one in the household is trusted to take a message, or to a fax machine which eliminates the answering machine.

Children are as bewildered as the spouse. There is suddenly a lot of talk about money and usually a tightening of the old pattern of expenditure. They are asked to hold strain until Daddy or Mummy makes it big. Usually they are dragged into the whole affair as supporting cast, who very often do not get paid. As a matter of fact their commitment to their parents, levels of gratitude and cooperation are all seen in terms of how they react to this new turn of events. The whole situation can become so emotionally charged as to threaten family life. Fortunately, if communication is clear and sensitive, and if time is taken to treat the players with consideration this can be a wonderful time in the life of a family, it can provide that lasting adhesive which keeps them together no matter what.

Unfortunately for some, in an already sensitive relationship, engaging in a new business may be providing pressure too great to bear. One partner may become jealous of the other's courage and determination and of the attention he or she may be getting. The partner in business suddenly begins to speak a new language, to meet new people and widen the sphere of influence. If the other does not keep on par there may be feelings of exclusion, and then nit-picking based on this jealousy ensues.

In summary then, your choice of business, will depend upon a number of factors among which are your:

- natural interests
- existing marketable skills
- access to raw material sources
- access to capital
- the demand for the product
- the market potential
- the level of competition
- personal considerations

The wisdom of your choice will depend upon whether or not you have taken the time to inform yourself, seek appropriate advice and demonstrate the kind of objectivity necessary for good decision-making.

4 Is This a Good Deal?

Opportunity Brings Risk

Entrepreneurs are particularly prone to involvement in various types of deals. Not being averse to risk, and being consistent hunters of opportunity, the energetic pursue every possibility with a sort of compulsion which might make them victims of modern-day carpetbaggers. The true entrepreneur dreams of the day when his small idea becomes a giant and seeks the quickest means to achieve this.

The modern business world is a complex place. Advances in the technology of manufacturing and communication, transportation and shipping services have led to unprecedented movement in financial resources, goods and services. Business linkages and networks hitherto unheard of are now possible, and the rise of service industries has increased the volume of interaction between businesses across national barriers. In more instances than before, capital is moved closer to the sources of production and new and unconventional means of creating wealth are generated daily.

The decision to enter into a business deal is never an easy one, especially when there is promise of high returns on your investment. Do you dare to let this opportunity pass pass?

Tread Carefully!

Your first task is to inform yourself about the person who is making the business proposal or if you are the proposer, the person whom you wish to enrol as partner. Is it someone with whom you have done business before? Does this person have a track record of honesty and reliability? You need to do some detective work on your own .

The stories of business deals are replete with unfortunate occurrences centred around dishonest persons who used half-truths and lies to ensnare the uninitiated and inexperienced.

Having satisfied yourself as to the good character of the person involved or, at least, being aware of what to expect, you now need to examine the legality of the activity being proposed. In countries like Jamaica where bureaucratic requirements are ubiquitous and suffocating, the temptation to by-pass the formal systems is very strong. Nevertheless, those who wish to do business over the long haul and who wish to develop a profile as a reputable company, should think carefully before engaging in any activity which may, in fact, be illegal. It is best to seek advice from your accountant or lawyer, in order to make sure you understand the implications of what you may be getting into. I trust you will choose to tread the straight and narrow however painful the process may be.

An Indecent Proposal?

Your next task is to examine the feasibility of the deal. Is it an indecent proposal or is it workable? Does it offer you an opportunity that you would not otherwise have? Some deals are straightforward, for example the purchase of a piece of equipment that might be going at a very reasonable price, or the availability of some scarce item in bulk over a short time-frame. Such proposals might constitute a drain upon your cash flow but may prove worthwhile if they enhance your productive capacity in the short term and allow you to recover your investment. If you decide that this is the opportunity you need, take time to ensure that the equipment or inventory item is of the correct specification and quality, and that it is compatible with your current operation. Never be in a hurry to commit yourself without proper inspection and testing of the items involved. Remember, white elephants best belong in India, there is no need for you to purchase one!

Not all deals are this straightforward, however, and many of them involve complex arrangements.

CASE IN POINT
Take the case of Harold and his partner who were engaged in the repair business.

They observed that with the increasing cost of new equipment a strong market was developing for the sale of re-conditioned equipment.

Refrigerators, washing-machines, air-conditioners and compressors were the main items involved. A friend based overseas, who himself worked in a repair establishment, hit upon the idea of making use of discarded equipment which needed minor repairs, by shipping them to Harold at discounted cost, in return for shares in the company. Harold and his partner saw this as a good deal, a chance to increase their sales and make a handsome profit. They approached their bankers for financing of the first shipment.

Harold and his partner, however, did not consider:

- the range of equipment to be shipped;
- the variety of brand names involved and the availability of spare parts;
- the difficulty of valuing items for customs duties, valuations being based on estimated market value;
- the availability of used items once the initial pool was exhausted;
- the commitment of the overseas partner to remain in the partnership for the long term;
- the basis on which shares would be offered. Once the items were paid for, what was the overseas partner really bringing into the business?

Here we see what was initially a good business idea coming to grief because enough thought was not given to the parameters within which the business should operate. Harold needed to have drawn up a proper business agreement which included an exit clause and which gave some commitment to a time frame which would ensure the recovery of costs involved. The act of committing an agreement to paper generally forces the type of thinking which will make for more feasible arrangements and better results for all concerned.

Dealing With Financial Consortia

Perhaps the most difficult type of deal to close is one which involves financial consortia. Here, generally more than two interests come together to mobilise capital for a specific activity. The place where capital and technology meets is seldom smooth and usually sees the flowering of self interest, enlightened or otherwise. The question "What's in it for me?" is a real one and one to which investors will require a satisfactory answer.

The deal, then, must offer some incentive to the parties involved in proportion to the value of their investment, whether the incentive is a share in ownership or returns on their investment – within a specified time – above what they would normally get from blue chip instruments. The greater the risk involved in the proposal, the higher the expected returns.

CASE IN POINT

Albert was an ex-army pilot, who chose not to be a career officer but to tread the entrepreneurial path to success. He fired the imagination of a number of fellow ex-army pilots and put together a proposal for a helicopter service for business executives as well as sight-seeing trips for tourists. They had the technical and managerial skills; they didn't have the money. They were fortunate to attract two initial investors of substance and contented themselves with minority shares .

Slow start-up activities and a number of mishaps affected this capital intensive activity, a characteristic of the airline business, and threw them into 'chronic working capital deficit syndrome'. They needed an additional injection of capital. They decided to go the venture capital route, not with one investor, however, but with a consortium.

This proved to be a negotiator's nightmare, as the powerbrokers were in fine form and any type of balance was difficult to achieve, despite the genuine goodwill of those involved. After much effort they were able to structure the new investments in such a way as to satisfy the new shareholders.

In situations such as these the technical partners have to be prepared to have the value of their shares eroded in relation to the total amount. Their leverage lies in the fact that without them there would be no business. It is a pity that financial accounting is not yet fully prepared to accommodate a true valuation of 'sweat equity'. Nevertheless, wise investors know that it is important to keep the technical people happy. It is not easy to see the ownership of your idea pass into more and more hands, but this is the reality of the business world, and you will do well to recognise that ten percent of five million dollars is the same in financial terms as fifty percent of one million dollars.

Which has the greater potential for growth?

The use of a consortium, then, severely challenges the issue of ownership and it is only the willingness to accommodate others in the business and to forfeit a great part of the control of the business that will enable a satisfactory resolution of the issues involved.

Franchising

From time to time entrepreneurs will encounter opportunities for securing a franchise. Franchising is a relatively safe means of entering a new business venture. In general it occurs where a well-established business give the rights to an individual or company to sell its products or services in a given area under its trading name. Well-known example of franchising occur with McDonald's and Kentucky Fried Chicken.

The franchisor usually makes available to the franchisee finished products, or standard recipes, formulae, methodology etc., and in addition provides technical assistance. Stated standards have to be maintained by the franchisee who is required to pay a percentage of sales or profits. This arrangement is sealed through a franchise agreement. The franchisee is usually required to meet start-up costs.

The business deal will become more prominent as the financial technology increases in sophistication, and the secondary market for securities develops. Increasing globalisation and the narrowing of the distance between cultural borders will all generate a mix of markets that will see products and services criss-crossing the globe, despite the establishment of trading blocks and protectionist measures. The successful entrepreneur must be prepared to meet the challenges and to benefit from the opportunities which await him. He must hone his negotiating skills and expand his knowledge base so that he enters into this rough arena possessing some advantages.

The main points for him to consider are:

- the character and track record of the person(s) making the offer;
- the type of activity being proposed;
- the feasibility of the deal;
- what other options are available.

5 HOW TO STRUCTURE THE OWNERSHIP OF YOUR BUSINESS

Whose Business is it anyway?

The question of ownership of your business is a critical one. You may feel that there is no question about it, the business is undoubtedly yours. The entrepreneur's dream of ownership is not to be taken lightly. Many people opt to run their own businesses mainly because a sense of ownership and the autonomy which goes along with it are important to them.

Today's generation have seen the scant returns their parents received for years of dedicated service, the inadequacy of pensions and the shrinking public sector job opportunities. They have also seen the gains made by big business, and the disparity between what top management and major shareholders earn on the one hand, and what the rank and file earn on the other.

These factors, coupled with widespread job insecurity in developed and developing countries alike, have had the effect of strengthening the yearning for ownership and the desire to hold one's enterprise close to one's bosom. The unfortunate thing is that many of the hazards of entrepreneurship lie in this very factor the issue of ownership.

Sole Proprietorship

Most micro-enterprises and new businesses start-ups, particularly in the areas of trading and the service industries, are sole proprietorships. The reason most often cited for opting for sole proprietorship is that no suitable partner can be found. One characteristic of this type of ownership is that often personal and business finances are intertwined to such a degree that differentiation is difficult.

Sole proprietors usually operate under a business name

which may be duly registered and assigned a business enterprise number (BENO). They are the owners of their companies' assets but they must also bear the responsibilities for all liabilities. For those who wish to operate independently and to be the sole decision maker, this type of arrangement is most suitable, particularly where there is a high level of informality in the business operation and where the keeping of proper business records is not seen as a priority.

Some sole proprietors wish to remain out of the formal system, seeking to avoid expenses associated with government tax requirements. As the business grows, however, it will become necessary to carry out operations in a more formal way, particularly with reference to securing lines of credit, loans and various types of insurance. Needless to say, even the most astute sole proprietor will feel the long arm of the law sooner or later as far as statutory requirements are concerned.

Partnerships

Another common form of operating is through the business partnership. In this case two or more persons come together to engage in specified business activities. Such partnerships are usually loose arrangements in which each partner brings a particular skill or resource to the business. In some instances there is a dominant partner, with the silent partner giving financial or moral support to the operations. Partnerships are usually limited to a maximum of twenty persons.

Business partnerships are fraught with difficulties. The strength of the partnership, more often than not, resides in the reasons for these persons coming together. Partnerships based on love and marriage and sibling links undergo severe strain, communication is undermined by other agendas, and suspicion grows if things are not going well in other areas of the relationship. In many cases these partnerships break down and the main player is left 'holding the bag'– very often a bag full of strange problems.

In one case where two brothers entered into partnership in a manufacturing concern the younger, who was the managing partner, refused to follow the business advice of the elder. He concealed financial statements and generally frustrated the efforts of the elder who had pledged security for the company loan. Such sibling rivalry can do great harm to the business.

Awkward situations arise when personal relationships break down and attempts are made to maintain the business links. Matters become worse when there are serious liabilities involved, with one partner bearing the brunt of these liabilities.

If your partnership is based on some ulterior motive such a holding a shaky relationship or marriage together, or exploitation of someone with technical knowledge or resources, then it is very likely to fail.

There are, however, partnerships which are very successful, where the balance between skills, resources and contributions to the business is maintained, where communication is authentic and the basis for the partnership is clear. The following outlines the features of a properly organised partnership.

1. It is normally limited to no more than twenty persons.
2. Any agreement made by one partner will be binding on the other.
3. A partnership agreement or deed is put in place, and the relationships between partners is governed by this agreement which outlines
   - the capital contribution of each partner,
   - the ratio in which profits /losses are to be shared,
   - the rate of interest to be given on capital,
   - the interest to be charged on drawings,
   - salaries to be paid to partners who are active in the day-to-day activities of the business.

It is important that a formal partnership agreement be put in place. This agreement should also state the basis for the partnership, the objectives of the enterprise, the responsibilities, and the contribution which each partner is expected to make. Acceptable exit clauses should also be included, so that there need be no confusion nor uncertainty if a partner wishes to withdraw from the agreement.

The Limited Liability Company

The wise entrepreneur who plans for business growth will quickly move towards the establishment of a limited liability company. This signifies the intention to operate the business as a formal entity which will qualify for relevant forms of business assistance and benefit from a broader range of expertise available through directorships and shareholder participation.

When considering the establishment of a limited liability company it is necessary to apprise yourself of the legal requirements. It is best to seek the advice of a qualified legal person, but a proper business counselling service will do just as well.

One of the factors which deter new operators from registering their business as a company is the cost. Legal and processing fees can constitute quite a tidy sum. In addition, processing time may be so lengthy as to discourage new entrepreneurs from attempting to go this route.

TYPE OF COMPANY

The first step in registering a limited liability company is to decide whether you wish to establish a public or a private company. Private companies can have up to twenty shareholders, while for a public company the number is unlimited. Most small and medium scale enterprises which do not consider being listed on a stock exchange remain as private companies. So, too, do family-owned companies which may wish to retain tight control of the enterprise.

It is important also to decide whether the company is to be limited by shares or by guarantee. Companies limited by guarantee are usually not-for-profit entities which are membership based and cannot in the future offer shares. This is a limiting factor for business enterprises.

Next, you must give careful consideration to the selection of initial directors. The law requires that at least two persons be named at the time of registration. Very often these two persons are family members, husband and wife teams, or close friends.

In selecting directors you should remember that they will

have voting rights and will have to agree to a certain share structure. It is wise for the principal player in the business to hold the majority shares. Fifty-fifty splits are not advisable, even where husband and wife teams are involved. It is very important to maintain the balance of power, as key decisions will have to be taken throughout the life of the business and serious problems can develop if shareholdings are not structured to favour principal decision makers. One important factor to note is that different categories of shares, can be offered which carry differing numbers of votes.

Sentiment should be avoided in the selection of directors. They should be chosen because the entrepreneur feels that they will bring something of value to the business in terms of expertise, influence and resources. Where the proposed business is family-oriented it is good to have a 'disinterested third party' as a director, preferably someone who is well versed in finance and who will bring some sanity to deliberations when they are threatening to become a family brouhaha. It is wise to begin with a limited number of directors, not more that five, an odd number being best to avoid ties in voting.

CHOOSING A BUSINESS NAME

Next, you must select a name for the business. One common strategy is to use syllables from the names of initial directors. This is guaranteed to give your company a strange name, although you may console yourself in the fact that it will be unique. There are those who go for abstract concepts like "Serendipity" or "Panache"; there is no end to these. For the more adventurous the choice can be enhanced by raiding French or Spanish or German. One word of caution, if you are going to use a foreign language, make sure you get the spelling right, and pay keen attention to number and gender. Remember also that there may be the perpetual problem of pronunciation.

Brainstorming among friends is a good way to come up with a name for your company. You will be amazed at how creative some people become after a few drinks. The important thing about your choice is that the name is important for establishing your company image, for motivating yourself and employees.

Make sure you like the name. Remember also that the Registrar of Companies will conduct a search to determine whether that name or one very close to it has already been used, so don't be surprised if you find yourself having to go back to the drawing-board in order to come up with a new name.

MEMORANDUM AND ARTICLES OF ASSOCIATION

The draft Memorandum and Articles of Association are your next big hurdle. These documents outline the aims and objectives of your company and state the activities which you will be legally entitled to carry out. They exist in standard form and may be modified for particular types of business. It is important not to make the Memorandum of Association too restrictive. It is better to go for a broad base of activities in the initial stages than to find that later the Memorandum has to be amended to accommodate new activities.

You should make sure that the Memorandum of Association enables you to hire and fire employees, borrow money and engage in various forms of financial activities. It must also allow you to rent, lease, purchase or construct property.

The Articles of Association outline the roles and responsibilities of directors, the frequency with which meetings should be held, the statutory requirements as well as other procedural matters.

A thorough vetting of the Memorandum and Articles of Association, despite the daunting nature of these documents is necessary. The entrepreneur should seek guidance as to the meaning of legal phrases and the implications of the various requirements.

INCORPORATION

Once these documents have been prepared incorporation is the next step. This is done through the Registrar of Companies. The incorporation documents are: **the Certificate of Incorporation, the Memorandum of Association and the Articles of Association.** The signatories on the Memorandum of Association are deemed to be members of the company and, as such, hold a specified amount of shares. This, in a start-up company with little capital is usually the minimum amount allowed by law. Shares can be increased as new directors are appointed.

And Now to Business

Your company, which is now a private company is ready to commence business. It is a persona in its own right and as such there are certain legal obligations which should be attended to immediately. You have already:

- taken steps to obtain the Company's seal;
- appointed the first Directors,

The Company should now:

- send to the Registrar in the prescribed form particulars of the Directors within fourteen days of the appointment of the first directors; any change must be notified on the prescribed form within fourteen days;
- have the name of the Company displayed outside the registered office and have it also on all letters, business publications, cheques, bills of exchange, promissory notes, orders for goods, invoices, receipts and letters of credit;
- have the names of the directors printed on all trade catalogues, trade circulars, show cards and business letters in which the company's name appears and which are issued by the company to any person.

It is important to know that you may wish to issue shares to another company, in which case the director representing that company is regarded as a corporate body and not as an individual.

Many entrepreneurs find it difficult to relate to directors in the company, preferring to have 'figurehead' directors who exercise little influence in decision making. In some cases directors are content to remain silent until the company starts to grow and make profits. Their sudden renewed interest can then become a source of annoyance to the entrepreneur who has almost singlehandedly brought the company to the position of profit.

It is wise, from the beginning, to ensure that directors are involved. At the first meeting of Directors they should:

1. appoint a Secretary. The Secretary's role is a very important one, it is his/her responsibility to ensure that all the legal requirements of the Company are met;

2. give instructions to the Secretary to obtain the necessary Minute Books and Registers;

3. formally adopt the seal and decide as to its safe-keeping;

4. appoint bankers for the Company and pass the requisite banking Resolutions, forms of which should be obtained from the Bank, signatories for cheques should also be appointed;

5. appoint Attorneys-at-Law;

6. appoint Auditors and give the necessary instructions as to the obtaining and setting up of Books of Accounts;

7. indicate the date of commencement of the Company's business;

8. authorise the issue of shares. You must remember that the shares held by the subscribers to the Memorandum of Association must be formally allotted either to them or to other persons and the appropriate certificates issued.

If, as is likely, they are nominee shareholders, then you must obtain from them:

(i) the signed undated transfer of their shares;

(ii) a direction to substantive holders (or in blank) to receive all dividends and other benefits arising from ownership of the shares;
(iii) forms of proxy (all of which may be prepared by the Company's Attorney-at-Law).

By now you should have recognised that it would be good to have some knowledgeable person, if not an Attorney-at-Law, sit in as a resource person at this first meeting of the Board of Directors. These technicalities are tedious but necessary.

You have flexibility, then, in choosing the structure of your company. Your options when summarised are:

- operating as a sole proprietor, you may choose to use a business (Trading) name;
- operating a partnership;
- registering a limited liability company.

Your selection of the form of ownership of your business is important, many businesses go through all three stages as stated above culminating in the limited liability company which offers the greatest flexibility for growth and development.

6 THE BUSINESS PLAN: A GUIDE TO THE FUTURE

An Essential Start-up Tool

The progressive entrepreneur should be wary of the various pitfalls which await. He should recognise when he is on the road to those negative situations which sap him of his vitality, and drain the business of much needed capital.

Let us take, for example, the matter of not having a business plan. Developing a business plan is anathema to most entrepreneurs. Even in cases where it is a new business, few operators give thought to going beyond the business proposal usually developed for presentation to bankers. There is a much used saying, "If you don't know where you are going, you won't know when you get there." This is exactly the case with many businesses.

It is quite possible that this avoidance of the business plan is born of a deep-seated fear that it may unearth certain harsh realities which the entrepreneur will have to face. Behaving like the ostrich, you bury your head in the sand and hope for the best (not realising of course, that it is when you bury your head in the sand that the most vulnerable part of you is exposed!).

There is also the fact of being penny wise and pound foolish. Many entrepreneurs fail to invest in planning, and in the long run spend far more paying for their mistakes. It is as if they are on a treadmill meeting crisis after crisis, finding it impossible to get off long enough to take rational action.

It is ironic that so many have a plan for a life in business but have no plan for the business itself. Operating without a business plan based on concrete data on the product, the market, the potential, and the costs involved, is to underdevelop your business and to do an injustice to your managerial capability. Of course, the same can be said for those who develop the business plan but operate without any reference to it.

CASE IN POINT
Let us look at Richard, an enthusiastic and creative entrepreneur. He made use of the growing interest in herbal treatments and medicines to develop several products with great commerciai potential.These products utilised indigenous herbs and provided a source of income for a number of contract farmers.

Richard's enthusiasm and congenial nature, however, were used more to sell the idea of the products than in selling the products themselves. He chased after every wild goose of a possibility for a new product, he refused to select those with the best potential to make his business grow until he had developed a strong working capital base. He had no structured marketing plan, doing most of this himself. He found that too much of his time was consumed in delivering his products and that, in fact, if he had a concept of a thriving business he certainly had no plan as to how to get there.

With a business plan in place, Richard would be better able to select, produce and market his products, maximise production time and capacity, eliminate wastage and build solid backward and forward linkages with producers of raw materials, marketers and distribution agents. All this would be a solid foundation for future expansion of product lines.

What is a Business Plan ?

You should, by this, be ready to consider your business plan. This is the point at which you seek to concretise your thinking and to put into tangible form the essential elements for business start-up or expansion.

The business plan is a technical document and is best developed by persons with the appropriate skills. The entrepreneur should, however, be intimately involved in the process so that he or she can begin to understand the essential elements that make for business success.

A business plan format is easy to come by and most of them follow similar lines, intended to guide the user into a properly sequenced business development mode.

The Summary

The plan, strangely enough, often begins with a summary. The summary gives a brief overview of the business to be undertaken, the main goods or services to be provided and the total start-up or expansion costs. The equity and debt components of these costs should also be stated. The summary also indicates who are the owners or proposers of the business and should state their past experience and in general their capability to run such a business. For sole proprietors similar information should be recorded.

The Objectives

The objectives of the business are next considered. Here the plan clearly states the reasons for engaging in this form of activity. Is it to fill a niche in the market? To provide a much needed service? To introduce a new technology? To support a new trend in consumer preference?

The Financial Information

The main activities to be engaged in are also listed, and a detailed costing of the business is provided. This enables you to compute the overall investment costs and to determine the amount of equity which you are able to contribute and the debt financing needed. It is important to state the nature of your equity and, if this is in the form of cash, what it will be used for. Sources for debt financing could also be suggested and a note made of financing costs. It would also be useful to give consideration to other forms of equity financing.

The impact of equity investments, including debt equity must be noted in such a way as to justify their use. The impact can be viewed through the eyes of increased production, enhanced productivity, or the capability to influence the market through the introduction of a new technology or a new product.

Ownership Structure

The ownership structure of the business is next to be considered. This will be of interest to your financiers, and should be of deep interest to you. You have first to decide whether to formalise your business into a limited liability company, in which case you need to register under the Companies' Act; or operate as a partnership or sole proprietor. In any of these cases you will need a business registration number. The relative advantages and disadvantages of these options will be discussed later.

Where the business is a limited liability company the share capital structure should be defined, the directors listed, and the amount of paid up shares stated.

Business History

The plan here reviews the status of the company, noting the length of time that you have been in business and your reasons for selecting this form of activity. For new businesses the latter is important. The business opportunity should be carefully considered here: what personal and environmental factors have led you to this place? Why this? Why now?

From here on the plan gets more pedestrian. The business history is considered next. For existing businesses this requires a summary of, and comment on, financial performance over the last two to three years, (so that trends can be identified), as well as appropriate forecasts for future performance. The current critical factors should be identified and the need for the proposed investment justified.

If the business is new, it is necessary to state the background leading to the investment decision, as well as a clear justification for the goods and/or services to be offered. Projected sales should be determined. For both existing and new businesses it will be necessary to calculate the break-even point – present and projected.

The Physical Aspects of your Business

Next, we must turn to the more physical aspects of your business plan. Here a number of questions will have to be answered:

1. Where will you be located?
2. Is the space adequate and suitable?

3. If most of your customers will be pedestrians, is it within walking distance of well-populated areas ?
4. If they are motorists will they have space to park?
5. Will delivery vehicles have access to your production area?
6. Do zoning regulations allow you to engage in these activities?
7. Do you have permission from your landlord? Do you have a rental or lease agreement in place?
8. Is it a reasonably safe neighbourhood for employees and customers?
10. Is the business area secure?
11. Are appropriate utilities available? (Type of electricity supply, water, telephone and waste disposal facilities).

These are some of the hardcore questions which you must answer satisfactorily in order to reduce the hazards which you have to face down the road.

Management

The management of the business is the next important point to consider. And here, perhaps a dream needs to be shattered. You may not be the best person to manage your business! This is particularly true if you are a strongly technical person, or if you are strongly entrepreneurial. You may have a conflict of interests. These will be between the entrepreneur who lives in the future, the manager who lives in the past and the technician who lives in the present. This is the challenge of the small scale operation.

There comes a time when both the entrepreneur and the technician must submit to the manager, especially the financial manager. If you find that you cannot afford a suitable manager, you should at least settle for someone to manage your finances, whether on a full-time or part-time basis. You will need the discipline and impartiality of a good financial manager to whose sound judgement you willingly submit.

You should develop an organisational structure summarizing job functions and stating the number of employees, whether full-time or part-time, and their level of skills. The gender break-down for employees is also of interest. The experience and competence level of manager and supervisor must be indicated as well. It is also useful to note provision for continuity in the business in case you become incapacitated or opt to relinquish the business.

Marketing

Marketing is the next item to be considered. Here, what is required is an outline of the market to be served as well as some evidence of demand for the products such as pro forma invoices, letters of intent or firm orders. A summary of market size and proposed customers as well as comparative information on the performance of the industry will enhance your plan.

Then follows a list of the main products, production costs and price margins, giving where possible comparative costs for other similar products or services. Yearly and monthly sales should be provided or estimates given.

It is important to note how the raw material as well as the finished goods will be transported and distributed. In fact a marketing plan would be in order here, stating what promotional strategies will be used, the costs attached and means for ensuring and expanding market share.

Production

We now turn to production. At this point you must consider the space to be utilised, the machinery and equipment, their suitability and capacity. Estimate the production levels and the percentage of capacity to be utilised. Indicate the sources of raw material or stock, noting their suitability, consistency in quality and supply and cost. Give an overview of the production process, noting turnaround time and machinery downtime. Arrangements for the maintenance and servicing of machinery and equipment should be highlighted. Provisions for quality control are also be listed as well as safety precautions where applicable.

Environmental considerations are becoming of increasing importance for business operators. It will, therefore, be necessary to examine the environmental impact of your business. Is your raw material renewable, for example straw or wicker? Is it non-renewable as in the case of marble novelties? Is it non-biodegradable like plastics or styrofoam? How will you dispose of waste material? Is there room for re-cycling, or a subsidiary industry? Will you be able to conform to existing regulations? What of the future?

Are You Breaking the Law?

You now have to give consideration to the legal aspects of your business as they relate to compliance with statutory requirements and other government regulations. Zoning regulations are particularly critical. If you are operating illegally, you may find one day, that you have installed expensive equipment only to be ordered to cease operations at that location.

It must be recognised that there may be some difficulty in securing suitable and affordable business space. In the absence of adequate suitably located industrial space, incubators and other facilities, many persons turn to residential areas to house their businesses. This opens the possibility of neighbours objecting to your operations and having these objections upheld by the law.

Appropriate registrations must be made and health and other operating permits secured. You, very likely, will have to take advice here as ignorance of the law does not obviate guilt.

...And is the Business Profitable?

It is now time to summarise the financial performance of the business. Here, profitability is stated and calculations are made of the returns on investment, liquidity ratios, break-even point and margins of safety. Some sensitivity analyses are also important, for example the impact of a 10% increase in variable costs, and or fixed costs, or say, a 10% fall-off in sales. This information should be supported with schedules such as cash flow statements, income and expenditure statements, and a balance sheet – present and projected.

The critical features of the business plan will be the

projections. These should ideally be done on a five-yearly basis and should indicate trends in sales, the various points at which new products will be introduced, capacity enhanced or additional equity needed.

Pluses and Minuses

Your plan concludes with a discussion of the strengths and weaknesses of the business. Hopefully the former will outweigh the latter! In identifying the weaknesses, you are, in fact, forewarning yourself of the possible negative events, and giving yourself time to develop a contingency plan for dealing with these threats.

To by-pass a properly constructed business plan is to expose yourself to the hazards of short term planning and short term solutions. You may find that you make grave errors in the selection of products and machinery, and may secure financing that you are unable to repay, when you have no properly constructed plan.

Entrepreneurial zeal is not enough, the business plan enables you to look at hard, cold facts, to determine the inter-relationships between different elements of your business. It helps you to do the mental mapping necessary to trigger your next creative thought; it acts as a guide and gives reassurance when the unexpected arises.

Revise, Revise, Revise !

To derive the maximum benefit from your business plan it must be revised on a regular basis, whenever there is a change in any element of the business, in the market response, government policy or in the economic climate generally. Your business plan should not be a secret document, it should be shared with supervisory staff, your business partners, your banker and your business advisor.

7 UNDERCAPITALISATION: THE RECURRING NIGHTMARE

The Challenge of Securing Capital

Research has shown that many small businesses suffer chronic undercapitalisation. This is perhaps, next to poor business management, the single most important cause of business failure. Very few entrepreneurs enter the business world from a strong capital base. Usually, they have had to seek debt financing either from commercial banks or through special funds for development. The less adventurous will seek to finance their new business from their savings or from friends or family. These factors invariably lead to under-financing.

The ability to adequately capitalise your business lies in your savings habits; your own nest egg is invaluable to start a business. It can be used as security for additional financing and is an indication to your creditors and other investors of your 'business-mindedness'. An accurate estimate of your working capital needs is essential and once it is acquired **there is no substitute for good management.**

All too often the amount of debt financing made available to a business, is driven not so much by properly estimated working capital needs but rather by the amount of collateral available for securing working capital loans. In addition to this, many sources of development finance either do not provide funds for working capital needs or allow for only a small proportion of the loan go for this purpose.

There is also the fact that, in the absence of a business plan and thorough analysis of projected income and expenditure, attempts at determining working capital needs are often inadequate. In fact **many business operators are not sure what really constitutes working capital.** The rather glib definition of working capital as the difference between current assets and current liabilities is only part of the story. The challenge is to define what future needs will be for one or more production cycles and to determine whether income generated in the short term will be sufficient to finance these needs.

A Long-standing Dilemma

Undercapitalisation is born of these two factors; ignorance of real working capital needs, and the inability to provide collateral to secure loans. On the other side of the coin, the matter of collateral remains an issue in development financing where agencies providing funding are caught in the dilemma of having to secure their own portfolios in the face of increasing financing costs, while at the same time seeking to accommodate the needy business with adequate amounts of money.

This dilemma has been long recognised, and has been an important factor in the development of venture capital financing schemes. Here the entrepreneur is encouraged to seek financing through equity investments rather than through debt equity (loans), or to use such equity investments as a means of enhancing the capability of the business to sustain debt financing.

In the case of equity investments, the investor takes shares in the business and bears the risk with other partners. Equity garnered through investments, unlike debt equity, does not require collateral. The entrepreneur who persists in starting businesses despite inadequate capital has very little chance of growing a successful debt free business. This poor start can lead to a type of chronic debt syndrome where the entrepreneur seeks to borrow his way out of each succeeding dilemma until the debt burden becomes so great that his assets no longer belong to him, or at worst, the business folds.

CASE IN POINT

Cecelia felt that she was ready to start her own business. Her plan was to rent factory space for the manufacture of ladies' clothing which she would design, and to offer these along with imported items for sale at an outlet located in a new high-rental shopping mall.

First, it was necessary to convince her that operating from two locations was not feasible because of high overhead costs, the demands on her management time, the volume of fixed assets required, and a market that was largely untested. She was advised to operate from the factory location only, in the first instance.

This was not a glamourous idea. She, therefore, made the decision to carry out small scale manufacturing in a back room at the shopping mall location.

The battle was not won yet, however, as she was advised against installing expensive fixtures and locating at this high cost mall. The amount of financing that could be collateralised covered mainly the cost of fixed assets, with an inadequate amount earmarked for working capital needs over the three-month period estimated for increasing sales to a break-even position.

By month two she had fallen behind in rental payment and was unable to meet interest payments on her loan, having received a three month moratorium on principal payments. With interest accumulating and rental arrears (the mall had in fact failed to open in time to meet holiday sales), Cecelia had no alternative but to seek rescheduling and an additional loan to purchase raw material to increase her stock of garments.

Cecelia's case is an example of the onset of chronic debt syndrome. Cecelia's dream was to own and run a classy boutique. She would have been better off operating from the manufacturing space in her original plan with a small showroom. She would then be able to put more money in the purchase of machinery and raw material and increase her production rather than having to use money for paying high rental, maintenance and electricity costs.

Guaranteed Customers for Life?

Managers of lending institutions recognise that some entrepreneurs will be customers for life, progressing from one crisis to the next, the decision being between those dual alternatives of rescheduling or an additional loan. Here the lending institution is getting in deeper and deeper with a dubious partner, not wanting to foreclose or having very little to gain from this route. Each additional loan is made in the hope that this time may be the break that the business needs.

There are, fortunately, those customers for life who make new demands because they have a growing business and because they want to expand into new areas. These are the ones who invariably made pragmatic decisions from the start. They were able to determine early in the day what size and type business could be adequately capitalised, and what options to use to get the business off the ground.

Cecelia could have been one such customer if she had not let the glamour of the classy boutique blind her to the reality of costs and risk and the fact that it is always better to creep before you walk. That is the way nature intended it!

The desire to start at the end, rather than at the beginning is truly one of the most prevalent of the hazards of entrepreneurship. Here, the chief culprit is the ego, the need to prove to oneself, friends and family that "I can make it on my own." Here self-image is so intricately bound up with the external social signs of status such as work location and environment, decor, and high visibility, that the more down-to-earth approach to business development is ignored.

Is Cash in the Till Profit?

Chronic working capital deficit can also be a result of ignorance as to what can truly be called profit. Some business operators tend to regard cash in hand as profit. This is especially true in the case of many micro-enterprises and informal operations where personal financing co-mingles with business financing. The day-to-day needs of the entrepreneur are met by dipping into the till. The food bill is paid, children's schooling is financed, additions are made to the house and the occasional holiday is supported by this perceived profit.

Entrepreneurs need to educate themselves as to what truly constitutes profit. The surplus created when income exceeds expenditure is indeed just that, surplus. When properly used, it finances working capital needs, makes provision for depreciation and replacement of machinery and equipment at future costs, and covers contingencies for liabilities such as inability to collect outstanding amounts. Statutory obligations have to be met and dividends considered, if it is a limited liability company, before there can be talk of profit.

In the absence of proper financial records, business

counsellors and credit monitoring officers are hard put to determine the real cause of the financial problems of the seemingly thriving business. In many cases it is the keen eye which takes stock of business surroundings and general living standards coupled with reliable on the ground intelligence which informs the banker of the nature of the diversion of funds from the business. This problem is so prevalent that some banks consider including family financial needs as a cash flow requirement when developing a project proposal.

Billing and Collections

Working capital deficit is often rooted in the high level of receivables faced by a company on any given day. You are not likely to be the exception, unless you are in the unusual but happy position of making cash sales only. Extending credit to customers is the norm for a wide range of businesses, particularly those in the service industry.

Convenient billing arrangements attract customers and stimulate repeat business. The entrepreneur should take care, however, not to make excessive use of credit sales as these can easily get out of hand, particularly when the length of time extended to customers exceeds that extended by suppliers.

Managing your receivables is rooted in good financial record-keeping, where information is available on credit sales with the date for required payment clearly indicated. Billing should be systematic and timely. The manager will then be able to determine which accounts are past due and contact customers immediately. The strategy is to apply the right amount of pressure so that customers will know that you are serious about collecting and develop the discipline of paying you on time. An *ad hoc* approach to collections gives a signal that you are disorganised and not serious about payment. Customers will take advantage of this.

In cases where there is a valued customer who is experiencing genuine problems some leniency may be extended, bearing in mind, however, that someone has to bear the time cost of money. In this case, unless some penalty is introduced, your business will suffer. The institution of a penalty for overdue payments is something to be considered, although most customers may not respond favourably to this.

The best strategy is for someone in the company to have the specific responsibility for collections. That person should be mobile or have access to a messenger or courier service which will collect cheques. This person, too, should have the benefit of specialised training in this field which will give skills in the psychological as well as technical elements of this area of operations.

Other strategies may include the use of pre-authorised payments, credit cards and special accounts. Every effort should be made to make payment convenient for customers; this will give you the edge in service.

CASE IN POINT

Betty ran a customs broking service. Her winning ways and numerous contacts placed her in a good position to increase her client base. The demands for a personalised service, however, and the absence of competent staff meant that financial-record keeping was consistently behind schedule. Customers were not being billed on time and worse yet, the management of receivables was not the focus of the company. The result? Chronic working capital deficit which crippled the business, as customs broking requires a considerable capital outlay.

The company soon accumulated a sizeable overdraft and was headed for serious trouble. Despite the additional cost to be incurred, Betty had the good sense to hire a competent financial manager, who soon had the billing up-to-date and set to work contacting customers and collecting payments on a systematic and regular basis. In less that three weeks the company was out of the red and in a position to make accurate projections for expanding operations.

In times of recession and slow economic growth, there is genuine difficulty in collecting outstanding debt. Small businesses are particularly prone to this as their clients are usually other small business persons at the lower income end of the economic ladder who are the hardest hit by the reducing value of money. In such a situation it is wise to go cautiously into the marketplace by reducing the level of credit sales, requiring deposits where possible and seeking out those customers who may be in a stronger financial position.

8 GROW OR BUST?

Is Big Better?

Chronic debt syndrome is closely tied to another of the hazards of entrepreneurship: that of too rapid expansion of the business. It may be ironic, but **it is when a business is growing that it is most vulnerable to failure.**

One of the first questions to consider when starting a business is that of scale. What size operation should you aim for in the beginning? There are many traders who start with little more than a few plastic bags, abundant energy and unflagging zeal. They prefer to test the waters – to see how they grow and to determine the market response and potential.

Such tentative beginnings enable you to become sensitive to individual preference and to personalise your market. You know what will sell and what won't, until finally, you can determine what the real risks will involve.

There are others who prefer to jump in at the deep end. This motivation is probably due more to ego needs than to achievement needs. "My business must suit my image of myself." This can be good sense in one context, and fatal in another. Pride has little place in the running of a business. Careful consideration must be given to the amount and type of resources which you will need for business start-up. The cost of capitalising a business will largely dictate the start-up levels.

Match Dreams with Resources

If the operation is capital intensive such as in garment manufacturing, for example, where expensive machinery is required, size will depend upon the cost of capital, its accessibility and the amount of equity which the new operator can garner. One thing is certain, if a business is undercapitalised in the start-up phase, this problem is likely to persist and to mushroom into greater and greater debt in relation to equity, and it may be virtually impossible to get airborne.

The size of your start-up operations, then, must match your available resources and must have the capacity to generate the level of sales adequate for growing your business. There are some entrepreneurs who make the mistake of not taking into account the built-in subsidies which their businesses enjoy in the initial years. They may be pleased at the level of 'profits' without recognising that by operating out of home, someone else is paying the utility bill and the rent. The use of a motor vehicle is supported by a spouse or a company. Such a person, when deciding to expand and perhaps seek a new location must consider the real costs of doing business.

The factors cited above are particularly relevant to a woman-owned business that is operated out of home and enjoys the considerable subsidy of a mate's salary. Such a business may have been started for therapeutic reasons, and has grown into a valuable source of income for the woman. To consider expansion, she must now determine real costs.

Some entrepreneurs continuously undercapitalise their businesses by using cash in hand to finance business expansion. In the case where strong sales are seen as an indication of potential for growth, many cannot resist the temptation to expand production, introduce new product lines or establish additional outlets without truly counting the cost. This diversion of money to untimely expansion starves the original business of cash and opens the road for serious financial difficulties.

CASE IN POINT

Ronald owned and managed a catering business. He started by delivering lunches to business places and catering for special occasions. Seeing the potential of this activity, he secured a loan to purchase an additional delivery vehicle, seen as vital for expanding his sales capability. All went well for a number of months until his banker noticed that Ronald's loan had fallen into arrears. Enquires into the matter turned up such answers as, inability to collect outstanding amounts on time, downtime of the old vehicle, and increasing cost of sales. On-the-ground intelligence, however, informed the banker that Ronald had in fact purchased high powered stereo equipment to provide music for parties at which he catered.

He was now running another business out of cash which had accrued to the original business. In the absence of proper financial projections as to the true cost of this new enterprise, and without properly identifying start-up funds, his original business was now starved of working capital and could not sustain its debt payments. Ronald was a prime candidate for an additional loan to finance the stereo business. Because of the strong potential for this activity to generate income, the loan was granted.

Ronald's entrepreneurial fervour was not to be curbed, however. In fact it was fired by the fact that he was able to secure additional financing. It was then that he embarked upon an expansion of his business site, which was adjacent to his home, to include a small pastry shop and a covered area where parties could be held. He was now in three businesses: the catering business, the party business and the construction business. Besides, all this was taking place in the face of growing family responsibilities, as his wife who assisted in the business was pregnant with their third child. Needless to say, he now had two loans in arrears as cash in hand was siphoned off to finance construction costs.

His bankers were now truly in bed with him, so the decision was taken to merge and reschedule both loans using new financial projections. This did not deter Ronald from purchasing a food wagon in support of his catering business. His rescheduled loan fell into arrears, but business was booming!

Ronald was clearly a victim of **chronic entrepreneurial syndrome.** He seemed incapable of resisting an entrepreneurial idea. Stretching himself and his risk to the limit, he created a nightmare for his bankers and very often had to sacrifice the quality of his products because of the complexity of demands on his time.

Not every compulsive entrepreneur has been as fortunate as Ronald. There are many instances where banks have had to foreclose, or where potentially lucrative businesses have had to be sold, simply because there was not the discipline of phased expansion. The entrepreneur must recognise that the accumulation of capital is an important element if the entrepreneur is to build strength to hedge against the risks of expansion or diversification.

Growing at What Cost?

Before embarking upon any business expansion it is necessary to count the cost. This cost is not only in financial terms, but expansion and diversification also have implications for the human capital as well. Managers of small businesses have heavy and diverse demands on their time. Very often they have to perform multiple roles which involve both technical and managerial tasks.

To expand or diversify the business requires significant portions of time which means that if the original business has not yet reached the weaning stage it will suffer and soon begin to show declining returns.

This is not to say, however, that there are not times when the opportunity cost would be too great not to attempt to seize the moment. Perhaps at times difficulties in sourcing raw material or in securing some component for the manufacturing process make it imperative for the entrepreneur to go into the business of providing these, some of which he may sell to other similar enterprises.

In some cases, it is necessary to expand production capability if the business is to achieve break-even point and move into a position of solid profits. In this case the banker is a necessary ally, as it will very likely be necessary to seek additional financing.

When to Expand

It is always a difficult moment in the life of the entrepreneur, the decision to seek to incur additional debt when in a loss position. It is at this time that the potential of the business has to be most critically assessed. **Financial projections need to be informed by sound knowledge of market conditions** which include a consideration of the general economic conditions.

Expansion or diversification in these instances may be necessary but not an ideal strategy. Expansion best suits mature businesses where the processes of production have been refined, quality standardised and the business shows some measure of stability. The entrepreneur himself should, at this point, be able to devote the necessary time and mental focus to what is, in essence, a new endeavour.

There are a number of clear indicators that the time is ripe for either or both of these strategies; for instance when there is growing market demand for the goods or services, where the business has found its market niche and has an acceptable amount of repeat orders, where customers express satisfaction and refer the services to others.

Another important indicator is when the establishment or acquisition of a business which provides raw materials or a necessary service would enhance production and customer service in the main business. For example, providers of printing services have long recognised that the sale of stationery enhances the choices being offered to clients and that photography services are extremely compatible with the mainstream printing activity.

The Role of Information Technology

Modern communications technology, with its astounding variety of computer applications, the increasing sophistication of the facsimile machine and convenience of electronic mail, has served to extend the capability of the individual to provide goods and services not only nationally, but across international boundaries as well. The concept of the world as a global village is becoming a day-to-day reality to those conducting business.

The technology will facilitate the maintenance linkages in a matrix of industries, promote the quick transfer of information and will lead to the more rapid provision of customised services. We have yet to fully tap the potential of the phenomenon of information networks and electronic modelling for products to be marketed.

The face of enterprise development is therefore changing, and operators of small and medium scale businesses are ideally placed to benefit from the innovations in information technology. A shift in technology, then, provides a good basis for expansion or diversification, provided that the culture of the business changes to accommodate its use, and that production can keep pace with the demands of high-tech information services.

Adopting more sophisticated technology can, however,

become a serious pitfall if the technology shift is not backed-up by state-of-the-art production techniques. The business environment must also support the new service opportunities being created by the use of information technology. The entrepreneur may find that he makes promises that he cannot keep and be faced with a growing number of disenchanted customers.

In summary then, to grow is not necessarily to bust. Growth can be managed where there is appropriate information and sound strategic planning. Growth which is too rapid and which opens the business to unnecessary risk is one of the hazards of entrepreneurship.

9 To Market, To Market

Many of us will never forget that nursery rhyme which began, "This little piggy went to market"... I don't believe that he was quite the prototype of the modern marketing executive, but one thing was certain, he was the most productive little piggy of the whole lot!

Many entrepreneurs are not careful to learn the difference between marketing and promotions, and fool themselves into thinking that broad-brush sponsorships, participation in trade fairs, advertising, and other high visibility activity constitute marketing.

Marketing Defined

Marketing is a sophisticated and disciplined activity involving product design, quality control, targeting of potential purchasers, careful consideration of how the goods or services are to be delivered to the customer, how often, and in what form. Successful marketing involves creativity and a sound knowledge base – creativity in designing those unique features which differentiate your product or service and a knowledge of the tastes, needs, location and purchasing power of potential customers.

Many entrepreneurs make the mistake of focusing upon the needs of potential customers without regard for their purchasing power. Indeed, **one of the hazards of entrepreneurship is the variation in the disposable income of consumers, particularly in a high inflation economy.** In such a scenario, sales figures vary reflecting the wide variations in purchasing power over time.

In servicing the market and planning production schedules

and cash flow, seasonality is an important factor: some goods and services sell more at certain times than at others. Those businesses which service the tourism industry are well experienced in the effects of seasonality. For them, strong financial management and some element of diversification are key factors for survival.

Few new entrepreneurs can afford market studies (and even where these are done, positive responses are no guarantee that potential customers are committed to purchasing your product). In many instances, in order to save cost, existing data bases are used instead of independent studies. These can, at best, identify trends but are non-specific to the business being proposed.

It is, in fact, difficult to determine the true potential of the market, particularly where innovative products and services are involved. The danger here lies in the fact that very often belief in the product over-rides good sense. This is more true when the entrepreneur is artisan and innovator and may be carried away by a less than realistic enthusiasm about the product.

CASE IN POINT

Alphonse was a small furniture manufacturer. He prided himself on his designs. One product that he was particularly proud of was the bed headboard, made of fine mahogany. Alphonse would spend an inordinate amount of time carving intricate designs onto his bed-heads of animal heads, foliage and vines. In fact, they would be a good representation of scenes from Shakespeare's *A Midsummer Night's Dream*. He was proud of his work, but needless to say potential customers were hesitant to purchase such overwhelming pieces.

Alphonse liked his bed-heads. He also had a passion for pie-crust tables which he assiduously sought to market, despite the fact that demand had shifted to knock-down tables which could be easily packaged for sale and quickly re-assembled.

Alphonse was not to be persuaded that a change in his products, based on a greater sensitivity to market trends, and less absorption in personal gratification were in his best interest. He was losing a great marketing opportunity.

Develop a Marketing Plan

If you are serious about your business, it is well worth the time and effort to develop a marketing plan. This will ensure that you plan your business with the necessary information, and may force you to face some home truths about your product or service. You may find that you have to vary these or change them altogether.

It will also give you a clear idea of what your competitors are doing and may reveal that your competitors are not necessarily your enemies, but may very well prove to be good allies to have in this age of joint ventures and creative consortia.

CASE IN POINT

Ruby was in the janitorial business. She had worked hard to establish herself, using her personal resources for acquiring equipment, living on a shoestring and ploughing back into the business all surpluses earned. She began to bid on larger and larger contracts and her customers were satisfied with the consistently high quality of the company's work. In common parlance 'she knew her onions'.

Ruby feared the larger companies in the business, until she realized that one company in particular, from which she purchased equipment, was willing to pass on to her some of its customers, having achieved the necessary economies of scale. Eventually, she was invited to bid on a very large contract along with this large company.

Not all competitors, therefore, are adversarial. It is best, then, to approach the market with positive feelings, seeking out opportunities for being creative and building useful alliances.

The Three P's of Marketing

Needless to say, the well-known 'p's of marketing – **product, packaging** and **pricing** – always require attention. Assuming that you have identified and refined your **product** and put in the necessary quality control, you may find that many a product fails to make an impact in the marketplace because of poor **packaging**. Packaging needs to be durable, yet attractive, and above all, it must be convenient.

One of the problems faced by business operators is the high cost of packaging. Operators of supermarkets and convenience stores are all too aware of the high proportion of costs to customers that can be attributed to packaging. Despite this expense, cheap, fragile, packaging is a turn-off to customers, while the opposite is a great attraction, particularly when trying to attract that type of customer who values chique or class as a way of life.

Remember, your packaging sells your business, it should be distinctive and should convey the type of quality standards which you wish to promote. In the mind of the consumer, packaging quality reflects the product quality.

Pricing is another important ingredient in the success of your product. Proper pricing is not an easy exercise; it presupposes an accurate knowledge of your production costs. This includes hidden subsidies, provision for unexpected liabilities, and informed projections bearing in mind inflationary trends. It also presupposes a knowledge of existing prices in the market place.

When introducing a product, or service which is new, there is a greater flexibility in determining the level of mark-up, which in this case will be more related to what the market will tolerate. The mark-up here will very likely to be higher than with a product where competition will have to be taken into consideration.

One of the pitfalls which face the entrepreneur is not reviewing prices on a regular basis, and where no proper records are kept the result is very little accurate financial information which is so necessary for proper pricing.

How Does Your Product Fit In?

For many entrepreneurs, particularly where a small business is involved, the market niche is of key importance. This may be determined by a number of factors. Geographic location is the main one, where the people served are within a well-defined radius and cover an area which is within the capability of the business to serve. In many instances, personal contact is important and enhances customer relations.

The competitiveness, quality, utility, durability and accessibility of the product are key factors in capturing and retaining your market niche. Effective promotion strategies will improve the likelihood of success of the marketing plan, and should reflect the production capacity of the business as well as the quality of the product.

With modern communications and the strong trend towards globalisation the whole world is becoming one big neighbourhood and your products may indeed have a market far afield. Because of this it is best to build in early in their development, conformity to international standards, unless of course, your domestic market is so strong that there is no need to look outward.

To be successful, **the market must be always on your mind,** you must be sensitive to trends and shifts in consumer tastes and disposition, and you must at all times critically appraise your products, their quality and their relevance in the light of advancing technology. Never take anything for granted, no matter how strong sales may seem now. Who knows? It may be that they could be better.

10 A Matter for the Record

The Importance of Financial Records

Research indicates time and time again, that one of the critical factors affecting the performance of businesses is that of financial accounting and record-keeping. Many people are of the opinion that this affects small businesses only, but this is not so. Large investment companies, multi-nationals as well as medium, small-scale and micro-enterprises are all plagued at one time or another with the negative effects of faulty or absent financial accounting and control systems.

In some instances business operators deliberately obscure records in an effort to evade paying taxes and otherwise complying with the formal system. For registered companies, this is short-sighted as, sooner or later, there will be need for accurate records, particularly when the company seeks financing, investments or assistance under some technical programmes.

If your financial record-keeping is non-existent or inaccurate, chances are that you will be a victim of the following:

- a high level of receivables: you will have lost track of your credit sales, and have no firm strategy for collecting money;
- the inability to identify hidden costs in your operations;
- poor cash flow management;
- misconceptions about the profitability of the business;
- the inability to monitor creeping increases in the cost of inventory and overhead costs generally;
- faulty billing on the part of your creditors;

- the inability to detect fraud and other irregularities;
- confusion between your personal and business finances;
- the inability to detect errors on the part of your bankers and other institutions which serve you;
- the inability to measure business growth and to determine the rate of return on your investment;
- the inability to comply with statutory requirements;
- the inability to make accurate projections for future expansion and growth.

Get Someone to do It for You

Very often, however, poor financial accounting is a function of poor business management, generally. The entrepreneur is a prize firefighter, attending to the myriad things that arise daily. Production, the collection of receivables, the management of staff, and maintaining good customer relations, all take their toll on the systems and structures which must be a part of the business operations if there is to be strength and stability.

Financial accounting and record-keeping require specific skills, which business managers might not possess and might not have an aptitude for. Perhaps you fall into the category of persons who respond to anything mathematical with a sense of inadequacy and even confusion. You might not have a good head for figures, but one thing is certain: to be successful, you will have to acquaint yourself with the processes involved in the proper financial management of your business. You will also have to put in place persons, whether staff members or consultants, who will carry out the financial function with due diligence and accuracy.

The matter of financial record-keeping is less problematic today with the availability of easy to use computer software to carry out calculations rapidly once data has been entered. Software applications now exist for varying types of businesses, and can eliminate cumbersome ledgers and errors in calculation. Of course, the accuracy of the data is vital, for the saying goes – "garbage in, garbage out" ('gigo', for short).

Financial Records for Decision-making

Many business operators ignore the financial function because of a failure to recognise the value of financial accounting in the decision-making process. This is particularly true of the chronic entrepreneur, who, seized with the excitement of a new opportunity, forges ahead on the basis of what seems like a healthy cash flow, only to come to grief in a short time. The keeping of proper financial records, then, is not a chore required by the state and financial institutions to keep you in line, but rather should be viewed as your own tool for making critical decisions and for growing your business.

The Balance Sheet

Many business operators, for example, do not recognise the importance of the balance sheet. This statement gives an indication of the company's strength, the value of its assets and liabilities and the sources from which the business is being financed. The balance sheet provides the basis for calculating the return on investment (ROI), as well as debt equity and working capital ratios necessary for determining the strength of the business. Your banker will request a balance sheet when making decisions for financing.

The projected balance sheet for example, will give and indication of the impact which the loan will have on the business.

Profit and Loss Statement

The profit and loss (income and expenditure) statement, gives the surplus or deficit position of the company on a timely basis. This statement can be used also to compare actual levels of expenditure or income with the budget. In this case the performance of the business can be closely monitored, targets revised and strategic decisions implemented.

Cash Flow Statement

Cash flow statements are important for the planning process.The cash flow statement enables the manager to determine the expected inflows, as well as outflows on a timely basis, and indicates possible deficits, the effects of seasonality, increasing operating costs and where in fact there will be a working capital deficit. It is important to note that this statement records cash only and does not reflect the value of fixed assets, non-cash equity, or the levels of depreciation and other liabilities which the company may carry. It is strictly an instrument for monitoring and determining the levels of cash which will be available for operations.

Other useful financial statements are the sales and purchases journals which provide information for computing the profit and loss and cash flow statements.

Beware of the Mix!

One of the great temptations you may face is the mixing of your personal finances with the finances of the business. Many persons argue that this is precisely why they have a business, to finance themselves. This may be so, but if there is to be sound business management and resulting growth, such 'dipping into the till' will only result in further confusion as to the true state of your finances.

Punitive systems of taxation contribute to tax evasion and business operators may seek to pass personal expenditure through the company. There is a danger here as proper auditing will bring to light any transactions which are legally disallowed.

Inordinate use of the company's resources for personal financing can have the negative effect of lowering staff morale, particularly where bonuses are offered on annual surpluses, and can also frustrate shareholders. Careful thought should therefore be given before embarking upon such activity.

Those entrepreneurs who find themselves in the unfortunate position of having no accurate up-to-date records should immediately set about to remedy this. Business counselling services are available at minimal cost, for assisting you to recover what data is available from scattered cash records, receipts and invoices. A good business consultant will be able to reconstruct records, and install a system of financial reporting which is designed specifically for your needs.

Training is also available in the use of systems and in planning activity related to the financial function. For your own understanding of what needs to be done and when, and in order to enable you to monitor activities, it is advisable to work along with the consultant and your staff to develop a schedule of job tasks. This should state those activities which take place daily, weekly, monthly, quarterly (if required), and annually. You can then apportion the tasks and establish the necessary controls, so that errors or irregularities can be quickly recognised and corrective measures taken.

The key to effective financial management is timeliness. A quick checklist will show that where there is effective financial management,

- postings are up-to-date;
- reconciliations are current;
- receivables are monitored and an effective system put in place for collecting;
- payables are made in relation to strict cash flow management;
- financial reports are accurate and ready at the appropriate time financial reports are used for decision-making.

Entrepreneurs who master the art of good financial management operate with a greater level of confidence, are more proactive in their approach to business and can, on the whole, exercise more leverage in garnering resources for growth and expansion.

11 WHAT OF YOUR INVENTORY?

Managing Inventory Levels

In operating a business, particularly a retail oultet or a manufacturing concern, the matter of inventory control is of vital importance. Your inventory or stock level, its quality and utility will indicate your potential for sales turnover at any one time.

Operators of retail establishments have to give careful consideration to the range and levels of stock to be carried. Here the guiding principle of good service may become the greatest pitfall as managers succumb to the temptation of seeking to carry a wide range of items in response to customer demand. It is best to make a conscious decision to limit your range of stock to those items which show a high rate of turnover, and to place on special order other items which your customers may require from time to time. In this way you can ensure that good service is maintained.

Your inventory is, in effect, cash committed to the business. If your inventory is too high, and has a slow rate of turnover, this is cash lying idle. The situation becomes worse if the stock becomes obsolete or if there is spoilage; this is money lost. **Careful selection and control of your inventory is of the utmost importance.**

The question of the optimal inventory level is a complex one and depends on a number of factors, including the following:

- the length of your production cycle;
- your production capacity;
- the shelf life of inventory items;

- the strength and seasonality of the market;
- the lead time between the placing of orders and the delivery of the finished product;
- the availability of the inventory items (where scarcity obtains, stockpiling may be an option but an expensive one);
- the space available for storage;
- cash flow.

Experience is usually the best teacher in inventory control. Here, the Manager must have a good intuitive sense of what is likely to be the most dominant of the factors cited above, and plan accordingly. A rule of thumb for the rate of inventory turnover for manufacturing concerns, for example, is twelve times per year, although obviously this does not hold true for supersonic aircraft or space shuttles. In retail establishments it may be much higher, depending upon the strength of sales. Energetic enterprises of this nature require daily monitoring of stock levels, both as a control mechanism and as a means of ensuring that customers are served.

Inventory control is an integral part of the processes of business management, and would benefit from the installation of a specialised computer programme to enable the proper tracking of inventory levels and the demand for individual items.

Whereas the aim is to avoid as much as possible having unnecessarily high inventory levels and dead stock, frugal inventory management can be taken to the extreme. For example, where orders are secured with no raw material in hand, the Manager is forced to launch a search for inventory items which may prove to be unavailable or of varying quality. This causes delays in the production of finished goods, and increases the risk of inconsistency in the quality. The result is many dissatisfied customers.

The availability of raw materials should be closely monitored and creative means used for accessing the cheapest reliable sources. Cooperative purchasing through associations and other industry groups can cut costs considerably. Care should be taken to compare cost quotations from various distributors, and not become locked into one supplier which may cause you unnecessary levels of expenditure.

Shelf-Life and Other Factors

The shelf-life of your inventory items does not only relate to spoilage as a pathological factor, but to style, taste and technology. Garment manufacturers, for example, must manufacture and distribute with keen regard for seasonality. Shifting tastes in style and fabric put them at the mercy of the designers.

Many a retail outlet may find itself saddled with alarming levels of what is essentially dead stock as the consumer moves on to the next fashion, or fad for that matter. In many instances gains from high volumes of sale of a new product line are severely eroded when set off against losses on the same line because of miscalculations as to when to pull out of the market.

How inventory items are stored is also an important factor. Temperature, humidity, exposure to ultra-violet rays, rodents and other pests, are all matters to be considered. It is important to have an adequate understanding of the storage requirements of the range of products which comprise your inventory. Some items are not compatible with others and might contaminate them; for example pesticides and other harmful chemicals should never be stored with food items. Where refrigeration is necessary, capacity becomes a factor.

Cultivate your Suppliers

A line of credit from your supplier is important for cash flow management, particularly if you offer credit to your customers. One of the reasons for a working capital deficit is the fact that credit time offered to customers often exceeds that allowed by suppliers. Such an arrangement is foolhardy to say the least.

It is important to develop a good relationship with your suppliers. By keeping the channels of communication open you will be able to secure inventory items with the optimum lead time and negotiate the most reasonable periods for payment.

It is also a good strategy to compare prices with that of other suppliers and to keep abreast of the availability of substitutes or new, improved brands.

Good inventory management then, involves giving careful consideration to :

- the range and stock levels to be carried at any given time period;
- keeping careful records of stock turnover;
- closely monitoring the availability of raw materials;
- safe and appropriate storage;
- developing a good relationship with suppliers.

12 THE PEOPLE TRAP

The Entrepreneurial Managers

The most successful managers are those who regard management itself as entrepreneurial activity. Those who, having digested the contents of the rule book discard it with confidence and decide to fly with the wind. Using their creativity, they make use of the air currents, the up-drafts and down-drafts and the supportive jet-streams. They fashion a positive environment for what becomes not so much the management of people as the management of results.

In entrepreneurial enterprises, traditional approaches to 'the management of people' can prove non-productive and may even be a distraction, diverting the company's energies from the real issues. Entrepreneurial enterprises face the challenge of creating a vision big enough for employees to see and follow, and real enough for them to feel a part of.

The entrepreneur who manages a business is likely to experience many difficulties associates with productivity, simply because of the nature of the business activity. He tends to be absorbed with the task at hand, the opportunities as they present themselves. Timing is the essence of success, and the ability to maintain a clear focus is his greatest asset. Entrepreneurial management begins with a clear concept of the desired efficiencies in the production process: the streamlining of each stage of production, the quality control check points, the motivation and training of work teams which must service each stage. In short, **the entrepreneur must be clear about what needs to be done, when, and by whom.**

Entrepreneurial activity is by nature results oriented, the shorter the time between the sowing of the idea and the desired result will be the sharper the entrepreneurial focus. Successful entrepreneurial management is characterised by goal-oriented behaviour by the total workforce. Where this does not occur, those employees become a liability to the company.

Entrepreneurial Employees

Entrepreneurial employees seek to stretch the possibilities to gain the ultimate excellence rather than maintain the status quo. They prefer to act independently rather than 'wait for orders' and they show courage in taking the risks that confront those who strive for excellence. Entrepreneurial employees bring the fervour of the big 'E' for enthusiasm, to their department or unit, they embrace innovation and change; and work for results.

The Word is Love

The word 'love' does not normally appear in management literature, but in the entrepreneurial enterprise the intensity of the human interaction, the singleness of purpose that must be displayed and the demands that will be made on employees' time and effort all make love an essential ingredient, and teamwork indispensable.

In any enterprise the performance of people is the core of its success or failure. Highly entrepreneurial activity requires a level of consciousness and know-how on the part of employees which affords quick responses to incidents as they arise. Technical competence must be complemented by good judgement, initiative and general motivational energy.

Very often the entrepreneur's greatest fear is how to deal with the people he employs. This is one aspect of his operations which he would gladly divest. And yet he must learn to deal with people. It is people who have created the need for the business, it is people who are the market, and it is people who will make the entrepreneurial dream a reality.

The decade of the nineties has seen a renewed interest in ethics in business and in the attitudes and values which made for a kinder gentler society. James Autry in his book *Love and the Profit Motive* writes:

Listen
In every office
you hear the threads
of love and joy and fear and guilt,
the cries for celebration and reassurance,
and somehow you know that connecting those threads
is what you are supposed to do
and business takes care of itself.

As an entrepreneurial manager you must first clarify your own feelings about people. Your attitude and your belief systems will colour your approach to personnel strategy. Your self-concept, your own feelings about yourself and your abilities will be the basis for your attitude towards others. Whether or not you accept your body image is also a factor, whether you are tall or short, fat or thin, black or white are all facts that you will have to come to terms with. In order to accept and love other people, you have to first accept and love yourself.

Picking the Winners

The new individualism will force you to think carefully about the people you hire. Do they have an entrepreneurial mind-set? The creativity and flexibility necessary for the kind of responses to challenges which distinguish the entrepreneurial from the functional employee?

In selecting employees it is best to hire individuals, not 'people for the job'. Start-up businesses, operating under a time constraint, often with little capital and no track record, find themselves with their backs to the wall as far as recruitment is concerned. The manager tends to opt for cheap, inexperienced labour with the excuse that it is all the enterprise can afford. If he really believes in the principle of hiring **individuals** and not people for the job he will find that there are exciting prospects out there and they are worth exploring.

The trick then is to go for qualities in your people as you go for quality in your product. But, what should you look for?

Qualities to Look For

Number one on your list is **enthusiasm**. Enthusiasm denotes a latent energy, necessary for good job performance. Enthusiastic people are curious. Curiosity is a basic for motivation. Motivation primes the pump for action and action brings results. The dull and the unenthusiastic constitute a drain on the emotional resources of your work team and make life a little less tolerable for all concerned.

Number two on your list is **creativity**. Creativity solves problems and opens up new entrepreneurial opportunities. People who are unimaginative are dull and lack innovative ability. They literally cannot visualise what would be the consequences if they spilled a cup of coffee on the computer keyboard, or what could happen if your company found a cure for cancer. Unimaginative people cannot make any real contribution to creative communication or the pro-active strategies you may wish to utilise.

Your third bench mark is **character**. By character I mean the individual's value systems. I recently had the experience of a young man requesting work. I had struck up a casual conversation with him in a downtown parking lot. He complained of hard times and having nothing to give his three children. I attempted to challenge his mind with the possibility of some entrepreneurial endeavour. He would not take the bait, however. I told him to come for an interview the next day.

I had no idea where this would lead, but was possessed of my own curiosity. He explained that he had worked with a band, had gone overseas and stayed on illegally and was subsequently deported.

This was a bad scene; it had all the elements of future trouble.

"The only thing I have to offer," I said, "is for someone to wash the company cars and tend to the window boxes."

That should certainly scare him off!

His response surprised me: "I'll take it."

I had to do a quick mental calculation, menial though the task was and poorly paid, he was willing to take it, to be employed, to begin at the beginning. Such an action tells something of an individual's value systems. Needless to say, I hired him.

What does the person sitting in front of you believe about work, about personal responsibility, about the children in Somalia? What does she believe about turning off the lights at night, or the eight-hour work day? Where do social programmes fit into her life and who should feed the stray cat? Should the company take gift packages to a children's home on a public holiday? And would it be best for you to keep your office locked whenever you leave the building? What do you do when you are left holding the bag?

If your prospect can satisfy you on these three counts – enthusiasm, creativity and character – that is good going, you can now look for a fourth ingredient: **the positive attitude**. There is not much said these days about the power of positive thinking, perhaps we are too absorbed with the development of new software packages, the FAX machine and the wonders of cable TV.

The last person you would wish to hire is a 'can't do' fanatic. A supporter of the hundred and one reasons why not. I suspect that the 'can't do' orientation is based in laziness, although it passes itself off as caution. 'Can do' people are positive about life. They see the value of rainy days and take a problem-solving approach to crises which occur from time to time. They are energetic and willing to go the extra mile to see that the job gets done.

It is only when you are satisfied that the prospective employee can satisfy you on these counts that you should look to certification, experience and all the other static requirements that characterise bureaucratic personnel systems. You may or may not wish to consider them. Remember there is a difference between the educated person and the certified one. Education will win every time. The person who knows how to learn is more valuable to you than the one who thinks he already knows it all.

Creative Interviewing

I am perhaps known for my unconventional interviewing style. In my personal philosophy anyone who survives my interview will be good for the job. Today's 'seminared' and briefed work force, at least at the professional level are so artificially primed for the interview that I make it my business to cut through this artificiality. Canned curriculum vitae and rote responses to standard questions can cause the interviewer to fail to see important personal characteristics which come through in the interview.

In order to give myself the best chance to connect with the individual I never crave isolation when conducting a job interview. I take telephone calls, I even make them! I respond to knocks on my door, introduce applicants to staff, offer coffee and share personal experiences. Sometimes I elicit comments on a current problem. My aim is to evaluate how that individual responds in an unpredictable environment. Will he go with the flow, or bristle with disapproval? Will he become flustered or be engaged in the process?

At the end of such an interview you will have a sound idea of whether that person could be the right one for your enterprise. Notice I said 'enterprise' and not 'job'. The thinking is that, if you hire the right people, you will find the right job for them. Their creative contribution to your company will make all the difference and will shape new entrepreneurial directions. The Japanese utilise this technique in some instances, where they hire with certain attributes, then train them for the job.

The Business Environment

Now that you have settled on the type of person you need to recruit, the question now is, what type of environment will you create for them. The culture of your enterprise will be a reflection of your personality and your people philosophy. Laissez-faire, bureaucratic, democratic, autocratic are all phrases with which you are familiar. Which description best fits your company?

Those of you who have been well 'seminared' will have been told at one point or another that you have to make a choice, and that it is bad to have a laissez-faire approach, except at the Christmas party. You should be autocratic only if there is a fire, and bureaucratic never. This, of course, leaves you with the one option which can ensure that you get nothing done. The trick is to be all of the above. The focus will be then not on your style but on the climate created by your approach.

The business climate must facilitate the entrepreneurial approach. Communication must be open and targeted. Employees must be allowed to question decisions, systems and processes. There must be room for trial and error.

There must be as little distance as practical between management and the front line. Theodore Levitt, in *Marketing for Business Growth* observes:

> All organisations are hierarchical. At each level people serve under those above them. An organisation is therefore a structured institution. If it is not structured, it is a mob. Mobs do not get things done, they destroy things.

This approach, however, does not work for entrepreneurial management. Entrepreneurs get things done by destroying the status quo and the entrepreneurial enterprise dare not become a structured institution. Structure absorbs energy, it does not create it, it diverts effort from the matter at hand and hinders teamwork.

Teamwork and Individuality

Although the focus may be on teamwork, it is important to recognise and come to terms with the increasing power of the individual. Naisbett and Aburdene in *Megatrends 2000* devote an entire chapter to the 'Triumph of the Individual'. In which they say:

> This is not an 'every man for himself' type of individualism, gratifying one's own desires for their own sake and to hell with everyone else. It is an ethical philosophy that elevates the individual to the global level; we are all responsible for preserving the environment, preventing nuclear warfare, eliminating poverty. Individualism, however, does recognise that individual energy matters.

The master-servant era is gone forever, the trade unions and social and political reform have seen to that. Entrepreneurial activity – legal or illegal – has spread wealth into the hands of the traditional working class. The growing numbers of *nouveau riche* have served to weaken the hierarchical class system and to promote a more equitable society.

This social revolution stressing the rights of the individual has implications for your entrepreneurial management style. Events in the socio-political environment indicate a greater assertion of individual rights, people are demanding more vociferously their perceived freedoms. The right to their sexual preference, abortion, freedom of speech, a smoke-free environment all have implications for the way you manage your enterprise.

Caution should be taken in the approach to teamwork. Teamwork should never be allowed to dilute individuality. Some people are not team players, at least not all of the time. This is not a bad thing. Few great innovations were made by teams. You have to know when to give an individual his head, allowing him to reach his full potential. He will be of more value to your enterprise then, than if you force him to go at the pace of the team.

The teams which work are those which are natural groupings around job tasks. **Team effort should always be about the tasks at hand and never about the people.** The best teams are vertical ones which follow the processes of production rather than lateral ones of people who are involved in the same tasks at one level of the enterprise. The idea of vertical teams is to build the backward and forward linkages along the production line, so that the standards of excellence are clear to all concerned, and each recognises how his activity impinges upon the efficiency of the other.

Many people have little opportunity to gratify their emotional, social and status needs outside of the work environment. As the wider society becomes characterised more and more by conflicting signals and confused norms, the face of home and family, church and community will change; the local Minister might be an avowed lesbian and your children may become alien beings. The workplace may become the only source of stability, and work the only balm.

An entrepreneurial business environment can offer the much needed opportunity for gratification of these needs. They may so challenge the individual that the concept of work will at last be given the elevation it deserves as expressed in the sentiments of the poet Gibran, "Work is love made visible."

Some Important Tools

There are other aspects of the management of people that are important in building a stable and productive work force. The field of Human Resource Development is becoming more sophisticated with the introduction of new methodologies in the management and development of the human capital in any company.

Experts in psychometrics have developed reliable tests from which can be compiled profiles of employees. They are also useful in the selection process, enabling employers to choose only those persons who show the preferred qualities.

Training is an area which warrants close attention. It is important to gather information regarding training needs, and to provide employees with individualised training programmes. The money which the company spends on carefully selected training interventions is well spent.

Disciplinary procedures should be clearly stated and ample opportunities provided for airing grievances. Disciplinary action should be fair, with consistency of approach maintained where cases are similar. Accurate and up-to-date personnel records are of critical importance. The Staff Handbook is a source of much needed information and should be regularly up-dated.

Although the company may have meagre financial resources, incentive programmes should be put in place which give employees an opportunity to gain some financial reward. This of course, does not take the place of recognition and other non-monetary rewards.

Regular performance appraisals can serve as sources of motivation. They set bench-marks for employees, help management to assess progress, and determine what is needed to close the gaps in performance.

Even in the best run enterprises, however, there are certain hazards which come with the management of people. A quick list of such hazards will be of help here:

- untrained or untrainable employees,
- theft or general dishonesty,
- subtle sabotage through actions like wastage, diversion of resources, faulty reporting etc., and
- absenteeism

The entrepreneurial manager will develop an approach to these problems and will find the best solutions which will safeguard the company's resources, while at the same time enabling the most promising employees the opportunity to realise their best capabilities.

A Final Word

In summary the entrepreneurial manager is one who is empowered to achieve results. He is so, because of the environment he has created for his business and the competence and attitude of his employees. And, because, together they take the risks, they believe they can achieve their goal.

13 YOUR BANKER, FRIEND OR FOE?

Banks are in Business too

Many entrepreneurs have concluded that next to government policies and regulations, bankers prove to be the greatest hazard. One thing is certain, you will not be able to escape either. An understanding of how bankers think and what motivates their behaviour is important as you seek financing for business start-ups, revitalisation or expansion.

Banking is a business in the same way that your enterprise is a business. The banker has the same concerns that you have. He must garner raw material (cash resources), commit to added value from which the cost of these resources must be paid, and provide handsome dividends to his shareholders.

He attracts deposits through building public confidence and offering competitive rates of return on cash investments. He utilises this raw material to produce a profit in a number of ways. He may lend it to other entrepreneurs like yourself, or for consumer purposes; he may purchase government securities and other financial instruments, stocks and other equities; or he may engage in direct investments in large projects in real estate, tourism and in some instances, agriculture.

The banker must be profit-oriented at all times. If he does not make adequate returns on his investment he has no business. His first thought has to be for himself and the protection of his depositors, because the money he uses is not his own. It may seem like a contradiction, but your banker is the greatest borrower!

The banker's focus is to minimise risk and to maximise returns. He is not an entrepreneur primarily, although he takes a considerable amount of risk. He must be ever conscious of the rules of the game. This is why he shies away from unsecured loans, holds your property as collateral, and is careful to attach stiff penalties for delinquency. The history of banking is one of somewhat ruthless action in times of recession and business downturn.

Your Banking Options

There are some disadvantages in using commercial bank loans as a source of financing for your business. Commercial banks are not entrepreneurial entities; most of the time they employ traditional techniques to achieve their goals. They can, however, provide useful overdraft facilities and demand or short-term loans for financing working capital needs.

The growing entrepreneurial thrust of modern societies has given rise to hybrid forms of banking with more flexibility in meeting the demands of new businesses. These have become known as 'near banks' and include merchant banks, trust companies, investment banks, lease finance institutions and various equity funds, some operated by insurance companies.

Insurance companies have probably become the most entrepreneurial of the financial institutions, making use of computer technology to design and market a slate of new products with interesting features that offer growth in equity for savers and access to this equity throughout the life of the policy. Some insurance companies offer pension plans and administer pension funds.

Income accruing to savings on your insurance policy can be a good source of equity for your business. Policies can also be used to secure loans from other sources. In some instances borrowers are obliged to take out life insurance for the duration of their business loan. Banks also have the advantage of insuring their portfolios against certain types of risk.

In order to select the best banking option, you must inform yourself as to the purpose of each type of financial institution and the services which they offer. You may feel a deep sense of loyalty to the commercial bank to which you have become accustomed. You feel confident in approaching the management and see them as being in your corner, especially when they extend a handsome overdraft.

In a liberalised economy, however, there is greater competition among financial institutions. Companies are forced to be more entrepreneurial and market oriented. You should seek to benefit from this. It is worth your while to shop around for the best package.

There are a number of things to consider when selecting a bank, among which are:

- its ownership and track record,
- the quality of the service which it offers,
- accessibility of relevant personnel,
- the type of loan package offered,
- interest rates.

For most entrepreneurs the matter of interest rates is of primary concern, particularly in an economic environment where interest rates tend to be high. There are a number of ways in which interest charges are computed. You should determine from your banker whether rates are 'add-on' or calculated on the reducing balance. Where rates are on the 'add-on' basis they are calculated on the principal sum loaned and apportioned equally over the life of the loan. Where they are calculated on the reducing balance interest is charged on the portion of the principal sum which is outstanding in relation to the length of time left to pay off the loan. In this way both principal and interest payments become less over the life of the loan.

Merchant Banks

A merchant bank is a financial institution that engages in investment banking. It offers business counselling services related to financial packages, mergers and acquisitions and organises various consortial arrangements. The bank itself participates in such commercial ventures and is, in fact, an equity holder. Merchant banks do not provide chequing accounts as commercial banks do.

Trust Companies

A trust company is usually part of a financial network that acts as a trustee for individuals or businesses in the administration of funds, estates and stock holdings (transfer and registration). Trust companies often provide mortgages and other long term loans.

Unit Trusts

A unit trust company pools the funds of its members and invests them in a diversified portfolio combining stocks, fixed income securities and real estate. Investors may opt for long term capital gains or short term cash returns or a mix of both. Unit trust funds are professionally managed and because you are part of a larger pool of funds, returns are higher than if you had invested on your own. Unit trust income is usually tax free.

Investment Companies

There are numerous investment companies which provide services to their customers through prudent management of their money, taking into account the economic climate. Funds are pooled to ensure the highest rate of return. You, as customer, will be offered a choice of investments and you should take time to inform yourself of your best option. The investment bank also provides counselling services to assist you in making your decision. Here again, the return on a pooled portfolio exceeds that on your individual investment.

Lease Finance Institutions

Leasing is a method of utilising assets by paying for their use over time. The company does not purchase the asset, but pays for its use on a monthly or quarterly basis through a legal lease. In some countries there are tax advantages related to leasing.

When the cost of the leased item is fully amortised (paid out over time), it will then belong to the lessee. Lease financing, strictly speaking, is a lease that does not provide for maintenance services, is not cancelable, and is fully amortised over its life. It is a useful mechanism particularly where there is a shortage of funds to purchase fixed assets. This mechanisms affords better cash flow management.

Financial Institutions are Governed by Rules

Financial institutions operate under strict government regulations. For example, in Jamaica, the new Financial Institutions Act defines the rules under which these entities must operate. The new act has widened the definition of deposits to include transactions utilising paper instruments and special accounts. In some instances these mechanisms were used to by-pass tax requirements.

Regulations governing banking institutions are designed to secure government's income from taxes on their operations and to protect depositors. Government's regulatory function includes strict reporting requirements, ensuring that adequate provision is made for bad debts and that the bank has the required amount of liquid assets reserves against a possible run on funds.

From time to time there have been cases of serious fraud affecting the integrity of banking institutions. The BCCI (Bank of Credit and Commerce International) episode is a case in point.

It is worth your while to acquaint yourself with the rules governing the financial institutions with which you do business. An understanding of different types of accounts and financial instruments is important.

The Current or Chequing Account

The current or chequing account is utilised on a regular basis for various types of expenditure. Deposits are made into this account and cheques drawn against it. The holder of the account is issued with a personalised cheque book which notes among other things, the account and cheque leaf number, the name of the bank and the branch in question. Current accounts may be operated by individuals jointly, or in the name of a company.

It is important to keep a careful record of the cheques drawn on your current account and to reconcile bank statements at the end of each reporting period, usually monthly. Banks have been known to make mistakes. Your chequing account can accommodate standing orders (a pre-authorised payment facility). For example, payment on insurance policies, loans and other regular commitments can be made through this facility. Your bank provides you with this service for a fee.

In some instances an overdraft facility is available, particularly where you are in good standing with your bank and can provide the necessary security. Holders of savings accounts with the same bank have an advantage here. An overdraft is, in fact, a loan and attracts a rate of interest which is higher than normal. This may become punitive if the overdraft is exceeded.

Escrow Accounts

This type of account is utilised when funds are set aside for a particular purpose, for example to pay mortgage fees or committment fees for loans. Escrow accounts may also be used to administer funds willed to a minor or otherwise to be held in trust. This type of account is usually a long term option although they can be opened for holding funds in the short term. In some instances these accounts attract a lower rate of interest and are bound by a written agreement. You should be careful to ensure that you fully understand the fine print in relation to funds which you may have in an escrow account.

The Savings Account

Savings accounts involve the use of a passbook which is a record of deposits and withdrawals. A savings account enforces some discipline and encourages the formation of capital. Rates of interest on these accounts vary and certain types of institutions, for example, building societies, offer tax free earnings on savings deposits.

A healthy savings account is a good indication to your banker that you are serious about your business and have the discipline necessary for prudent management of your financial affairs. Savers are seen as better risks than non-savers.

Useful Financial Instruments

There are a number of financial instruments which are useful when seeking financing for your business operations. **A promissory note** is given to a provider of cash for a specific purpose. The note promises to make good payment in a period of time and at a rate of return which is specified. Bank loans are executed using promissory notes; they usually do not exceed ninety days in duration. The borrower may be required to maintain a certain balance in his chequing account to compensate for the issuing of the promissory note.

Debentures are issued as a form of security and may be used to access cash. For example, when a loan is approved the bank may decide to take a debenture on the assets of the company which will be disposed of in case of default. Debentures and promissory notes may be passed on to a third party who assumes the liability. They can also be renegotiated. Debentures can also be converted to equity in the business.

A **letter of credit** is an instrument used to make payment to the producer of goods or services with the understanding that the issuer will be provided with the agreed amount of the product at a stated time. Letters of credit may be discounted by a third party such as a merchant bank, if the company is strapped for cash. The discount facility provides an agreed percentage of the total letter of credit at an agreed rate of interest. The period given for repayment is usually for the duration of the letter of credit.

Development Finance Institutions (DFIs)

This group consists of institutions which have been designed to provide specialised financing for productive activity and infrastructural development. They have flourished in developing countries and have been the main channel for disbursement of loans from international development agencies. They are essentially of two types: **public sector DFIs** are totally government owned, while **private sector DFIs** attract private capital or a mix of public and private equity.

Public sector DFIs have fallen from grace somewhat with the major international development finance agencies. The World Bank, for example, cites abuse of bank funds by politically motivated interests in Asia and Africa as the main reasons for poor repayment rates and lack of impact on economic growth.

The thinking has been that because these entities offer financing at concessionary rates, they act as a magnet for unscrupulous persons with ill-conceived and uncompetitive projects, and are used to provide inordinate levels of support to government-backed projects with little provision for accountability and no guarantee of their continuation when the political directorate changes.

Policies of DFIs

The international lending agencies have been most stringent in their demands on DFIs and have linked loans and other forms of assistance with the implementation of certain fiscal and monetary policies. In Jamaica, public sector DFIs, in response to conditionalities attached to loans from the International Monetary Fund (IMF), are no longer able to provide subsidised credit but must ensure that money reaches end users at 'market rates'.

The main concern of funding agencies is the sustainability of these lending institutions and the fact that sources of funding at concessionary rates of interest are often abused and create unfair competition in a market economy.

Private sector DFIs have more flexibility in determining their loan policy. They enjoy special status as venture capital institutions, but like other development banks, they do not take deposits.

If you take the time to investigate you will find that a number of funds are available for financing small businesses and micro-enterprises. These will be useful to you, particularly in the start-up phase as they offer specialised services.

The Advantage of DFIs

If your enterprise is part of the productive sector, that is, one which creates added value with the finished product, and generating employment in the process, you will qualify for assistance from development funds.

DFIs operate differently from other banks. There are often complaints of the length of time it takes to have loans approved, and the amount of documentation which is required before a proposal will be considered.

It must be noted that the operating word for these banks is 'development', that is their mission. Part of their task is to motivate their clients to develop good business skills. A development banker is not content to lend money, take collateral and wish the borrower luck. Many entrepreneurs miss the point: the song and dance about financial projections, evidence of market, soundness of product and technical skills is primarily for their benefit. It is designed to take the scales from eyes blinded by entrepreneurial zeal and to promote the use of the tools necessary for business success.

DFIs provide customised services. When you approach a DFI you enter into a partnership, one through which your business skills will be sharpened and one which will enable you to plan your business development from a greater knowledge base.

This is not to deny, of course, that many DFIs are slow-moving and highly bureaucratic. Their tardiness is a hazard to entrepreneurship. This has caused many entrepreneurs to miss valuable opportunities and to suffer increased costs as a result. In fact, tardiness in loan approval is a contributor to under-capitalisation of your business, particularly in a macroeconomic climate characterised by high inflation.

The Loan Proposal

There are two basic approaches to your DFI. One is for business advice. You may wish to explore entrepreneurial possibilities, determine what are the growth areas and see how your interests and capabilities fit the going mix. The second is for financing for business start-up or expansion. In this case you should gather the necessary information beforehand. The following will most likely be required for your loan proposal:

- *Historical financial records.* If these are not accurate and up-to-date a business counselling service can assist you in constructing such records with reasonable accuracy.

- *The purpose for which financing is sought* should be clear in your mind, although this may be subject to modification as your loan proposal is developed. Most loans involve a mix of financing for fixed assets, (machinery and other equipment), and working capital (to purchase raw material and cover overheads). DFIs traditionally do not favour working capital loans, preferring to rely upon the entrepreneurs own resources for financing operations. This approach, is, however, changing as working capital needs escalate and the cost of doing business far outstrips the entrepreneur's capability to accumulate capital.

- *The existing and potential market* should be identified. Orders should be supported by pro-forma invoices where available and evidence of the acceptable quality of your products. A comment on prevailing market conditions and the strength of competition should also be included.

- *The sources of raw material* should be named with evidence of consistency of supply or possible alternatives in case your named source fails.

- Information must also be provided to indicate *the technical competence of management and labour.*

- The proposal must give a clear picture of *the process of production,* including the number and variety of units to be produced over a specified time period. Unit costing should be noted and the level of mark-up to be applied stated.

- Perhaps the most difficult part of your proposal will be *the financial projections.* A balance sheet will have to be constructed and projected cash flows over the life of the proposed loan computed. An income and expenditure statement is also useful. The project officer assigned to you by the bank will undertake the main responsibility for these and will also undertake the computation of other financial indicators such as the break-even point, return on investment, and debt-equity ratio. Be prepared to make available your *personal affairs statement.* This will give and indication of your net worth.

- Finally, you cannot escape that controversial issue: *the matter of collateral.* DFIs are characterised by their flexible collateral requirements. The collateral required is more closely related to project viability than to the amount borrowed, and may range from bills of sale on equipment purchased, to liens on real estate. Personal guarantees will also be accepted.

Your development bank will have other interests in the growth and development of your enterprise. It will very likely provide a wide range of training programmes, seminars, workshops, individualised business counselling and consultancy services. Information services are also available on new investment opportunities, improved technology, and marketing possibilities. The wise entrepreneur will seek to take advantage of these services.

Remaining on the Right Side of Your Banker

Once your loan application to any financial institution is approved, it is in your best interest to ensure that you follow your repayment schedule and so not fall into arrears.

It will be necessary for you to fulfill the conditions of the loan before disbursement begins. This will involve signing the **loan agreement** which, depending on the institution, may be the same as the letter of offer. Depending on the nature of the collateral to be used, bills of sale or mortgages have to be registered, debentures and liens noted. A lien is a charge on property or commodity which is registered in the name of the lender.

One serious hazard to entrepreneurship is misuse of funds borrowed. Disbursements on your loan should be used only for the purposes stated in the loan proposal. Diversion of funds will have the effect of undercapitalising your business thereby reducing your capacity to earn, and is a sure prescription for falling into arrears.

Funds disbursed by your bank may be paid out to third parties, for example suppliers of raw materials or equipment. Where there is some element of re-financing (paying out of existing debt), disbursements may go to another financial institution. It is important to keep your banker informed as to the progress of the business. If you are experiencing difficulties in repaying the agreed amounts because productivity is below the expected levels, you may wish to request a rescheduling of your loan over a longer period, and reduce the size of regular payments.

In some cases of rescheduling, outstanding interest charges may be capitalised, that is, added to the original principal amount borrowed. This increases the size of your loan but allows you to repay over a longer period.

If your banker decides to call in your loan, it is an indication that he is convinced that the conditions of the loan will never be met or that you have broken some aspect of the agreement. Such a situation can be avoided if the bank is kept abreast of important issues relating to your business. You may get useful advice on preventive measures which can be taken.

A Friend It Is!

Your banker can be the best friend to your business. The relationship between entrepreneur and banker is no different from any other human relationship where good communication is predicated upon trust, integrity and mutual self-interest. Remember, not every entrepreneur is as honest as you think you are. Your banker has his own story to tell for there are hazards peculiar to his brand of entrepreneurship. It will therefore be important for you to build his confidence in you as an honest entrepreneur.

14 VENTURE CAPITAL, THE ROUTE TO HAPPINESS?

I regard venture capital financing as sufficiently important to warrant separate treatment. Narrowly defined, venture capital is a private source of capital for a high-risk business activity. The capital is obtained through the sale of shares in the business with the promise of high returns within a specified time frame. The time delay in the pay-out of dividends on shares is computed so as to allow the business to turn over resources at a high enough level to facilitate its own capital formation.

Venture capital of this nature is considered as equity financing since investments are unsecured. The venture capitalist is prepared to share the risk with the entrepreneur in return for part ownership of the business.

Equity investments are distinguished from debt equity in that the latter is a loan and is secured, in whole or in part, by various forms of collateral and does not involve the sale of shares. Some financial institutions, mainly development finance institutions provide venture loans which are essentially high-risk investments. They are characterised by an emphasis on business viability and high rates of return, rather than on the collateral available. With venture loans, the bank is prepared to take more risk than normally.

Commercial banks, as a rule, do not engage in venture capital financing. This form of financing is usually done through trust companies or merchant banks, or in an indirect form, through lease financing arrangements. There is a range of paper instruments, however, such as debentures and promissory notes which equate to venture capital investments although there is no formal purchase of shares.

Why Venture Capital?

What is the thinking behind venture capital schemes? They provide a mechanism for the mobilisation of much needed capital for the growing entrepreneurial trend. The venture capital mechanism serves the vital function of **linking capital to production.**

In these closing years of the twentieth century we face the phenomenon of the growth of the financial industry. Money has itself become a commodity; financial technology and the development of computer software have facilitated cross-border trading in financial instruments. The interplay of dollar, yen, deutschmark, franc and pound sterling is so intense and dynamic that it may not be long before a single world currency is introduced. The venture capitalist is seeking to use the new opportunities to generate real wealth.

Venture Capitalists are Risk-Takers

The history of private venture capital schemes is not a happy one. The period of intense activity in the sixties and seventies was characterised by heavy speculation, with the focus more on mobilising money, than on sound business ideas. The thinking was: the greater the risk, the greater the possibility of high returns. Venture capital financing in many instances became little more than a game of chance. Today, as a result of their past experiences, venture capital facilities are settling for a more realistic approach to this form of investment.

At the time of writing, venture capital firms in the USA reported a negative annual return over the last six years, averaging fifteen to sixteen percent on their twenty-year investments. In venture capital circles there is what is known as the '2:6:2' rule. That is, all things being equal, in every ten venture capital investments, two are likely to do very well, six may be described as 'marginal to poor' and the remaining two will 'blow your toes up'. The trick is for the last two not to be a significant part of the portfolio.

The Best Route?

Despite the negative experiences, venture capital investments, when properly designed and competently managed, offer the best alternative financing for the implementation of an entrepreneurial idea where there is a shortage of capital. Debt financing has the effect of draining the company's earnings in the short term, and in economies where high interest rates prevail, the cost of debt servicing may be more than the income the company is able to generate. In some instances the business is already heavily indebted and is unable to attract additional loans.

Types of Venture Capital Financing

Venture capital financing can take a number of forms. **Seed capital** may be necessary in the start-up stages of the business. At this point there may be little more than a business plan. Funding may be necessary for a feasibility study; if this cannot be obtained through a specialised facility, seed capital can be used for this purpose. It is also used for product development and marketing. Businesses up to a year old or more, which in real terms have not yet mobilised resources, can qualify for seed capital.

From the point of view of the venture capitalist, the provision of seed capital carries higher risk than other forms of venture capital investments. It is for this reason that venture capitalists prefer one hundred per cent equity financing at this stage to avoid a heavy debt burden. Seed capital need not only be accessed though formal venture capital schemes. In fact, much of this form of investment is garnered through individuals and small groups.

A second type of venture capital investment is known as **bridge or mezzanine financing.** At this stage the business requires financing for the purchase of buildings, fixed assets, property, equipment, the increase of inventory and general working capital needs. The venture capitalist is on safer ground here, because of the reduced risk based on previous performance and because of the expected fast expansion and growth in the short term.

Bridge or mezzanine financing is usually a precursor to a public offer of shares in the company and venture capitalists will seek to cash in on the benefits before this next phase is embarked upon. Because of this it may be regarded as a quick 'in and out' form of investment.

Venture capital facilities also provide funds for refinancing and turnaround activities in cases where a good business suffers from chronic undercapitalisation, or faces some critical incident.

Do You Need Venture Capital?

You may not be able to identify sources of financing for your new entrepreneurial idea. Debt financing might not be available to you for reasons varying from the high interest rates, high risk in the start-up phase, to absence of sufficient collateral. Your own financial resources may be inadequate, or you may be unwilling to invest all your nest egg in the new endeavour. If your idea is a sound one and promises reasonable returns in the medium term you are a prime candidate for venture capital investment.

On the other hand you may have already started operations with your own investments and some debt equity. The growth rate of the business has been steady and offers a clear opportunity for expansion. Equity financing is a sound option for moving into this expansion as it obviates the need for further expensive debt financing.

Unhappily you may be one of those with a good business gone sour through no fault of your own. If this is the case, you would be well advised to pursue venture capital investment opportunities with vigour. This, I assure you, is not the venture capitalists' favourite form of investment. They will take some persuading.

Managers of venture capital funds are trained to have an eagle eye both for the opportunities your proposal presents and the pitfalls. They will not be mesmerized by flashy presentations or promises of staggering rates of return on investment. They arrive at their decision to invest after much consideration and after safe-guarding their investment through careful screening of applicants and thorough negotiations relating to the volume and type of shares to be acquired, ensuring that their participation is not only in ownership but in management. They also consider and weigh carefully fellow investors and place high on the agenda the management expertise to be applied to the business.

Do I Want to Share Ownership of my Business?

I have left the most critical point for last. It is the point at which most entrepreneurs turn on their heels and walk away from venture capital investments. It is the matter of someone else owning part of your business.

Most entrepreneurs are possessive. They covet the ownership of their business. They have a latent fear of being bought out or of losing control to other persons who may own capital but have no expertise. They are afraid of losing their idea, that part of themselves that constitutes the business. This possessiveness is one of the hazards of entrepreneurship.

In some instances the fear of admitting new partners is because of a reluctance to meet the statutory requirements, and to pay taxes on profits. Where there is a venture capital partner, operations must be transparent, board representation clarified and meetings held regularly.

The modern entrepreneur who is heading for the twenty-first century recognises that in order to grow, his business cannot be operated as a private club. He knows that the growing and selling of businesses is itself a business and in this sense he can become the greatest venture capitalist of all! The entrepreneur who thinks of the future knows that businesses may come, and businesses may go, but if he is smart, he can go on from business to successful business.

To Sum up

Overcome your fear and face the possibility of a venture capital investment with confidence.

15 Government Policy and Regulations

The Entrepreneurial Environment

The greatest hazard to entrepreneurship is an inefficient, misinformed and overly bureaucratic government, where policies operate more in terms of putting rules and regulations in place and taking punitive action when these are breached, than to encourage entrepreneurs to go into business and help their businesses to grow.

Entrepreneurship will not thrive where government policy and regulations restrict private enterprise. The free movement of capital, goods and people is essential in building a healthy business climate.

One of the primary concerns of international development agencies is that governments whom they assist should adopt the principles of democracy and allow for the sort of political environment which promotes freedom of choice. These agencies, through their structural adjustment programmes, favour private enterprise and promote the private sector as the 'engine of growth'. The role of government in countries which operate under such an agreement with the International Monetary Fund, is diminishing. State owned entities such as banks and airlines are being divested, and the base of private sector ownership is being widened.

This has created greater opportunities for entrepreneurs. Those who are able to mobilise the capital necessary, or to access various types of consortial arrangements, can now have ownership in these newly divested enterprises and work to move them into greater efficiency.

Private sector initiatives, however, work best in countries where there is a clearly articulated industrial policy, where monetary and fiscal strategies are compatible with the growth of productive enterprises.

A Good Infrastructure Promotes Entrepreneurship

For businesses to thrive there must be the necessary infrastructure. Road networks must be adequate for the movement of raw materials and finished products. Businesses which operate in rural areas are very often at a disadvantage because of poor road and rail links, and the resultant higher cost of moving their goods compared with those businesses operating in the metropolitan areas.

Shipping services also need to be adequate. Air and sea links form an important part of the cost structure of export businesses. Where such links are relatively cheap and operate on an acceptable time schedule, they can make the difference in the cost at which the finished product reaches the market. If you are in the export business you must take time to determine the best form of shipping. The services of a good customs broker are invaluable here. This can save you time and money.

An appropriate and reliable supply of electricity is another important infrastructure need. Power outages lead to expensive down-time, costly and sometimes irreparable damage to machinery. Some manufacturing activities require more than a domestic supply of electricity and have to be specially wired. It is worth your while to find out if the supply of electricity at your proposed business site will be adequate for your needs.

CASE IN POINT

A sad reminder of the importance of this is the case of Ian who had received financing to set up a plant to manufacture lunch boxes. His factory was located some distance away from his major buyers and the cost of fixed assets (equipment and machinery) was very high. Ian had overlooked the matter of the electricity supply. As it turned out, he needed to install a voltage level that was not available on the site. The length of time taken to install the necessary 'three-phase' current delayed the starting time of the business to the extent that his loan fell into arrears and eventually he had to sell the newly purchased equipment to recover his losses.

Telephones and other telecommunications linkages are a must in a modern business. These should be available to you at reasonable cost. Such facilities allow you to place orders and access buyers as the need arises. They also give you access to important information enabling you to make timely decisions.

The matter of industrial space is the concern of government. Where zoning laws restrict business operations, attention must be given to providing suitable industrial complexes where there may be shared services, and where rentals or leases are at reasonable rates. Where government may not wish to bear the total cost of these facilities, public/private sector partnerships should be explored.

Social Conditions

One of the hazards of entrepreneurship is crime. For big businesses and small businesses alike, the cost of security systems can be a burden. Where social conditions lead to high levels of crime and social unrest, business operations are threatened. This is compounded by the fact that business districts are often found close to poor neighbourhoods and ghetto areas where the crime rate is higher. Where governments are not able to implement effective controls on crime and to institute social and economic programmes for the revitalisation of poor communities, the survival of businesses in these areas is threatened.

Small-scale and micro-enterprises are particularly vulnerable to neighbourhood 'dons' who may demand protection money, or to frequent robberies. These businesses which are unable to provide their own security services require adequate policing of areas where they are located.

The Labour Force

As the worker becomes more and more at the centre of productive activity Human Resource Development will be a key factor in economic growth. The quality and relevance of education and training will make the difference in the productivity of the work-force.

Education and training are the pillars upon which entrepreneurship is built. Without thinkers, technicians, and professionals the entrepreneurial process will stagnate. Governments must take responsibility for monitoring manpower needs and ensuring that the necessary education and training services are delivered whether by government alone in some cases or in partnership with private entities in others.

Governments must focus on the financing of education and on curriculum development. The training needs of the labour force must be high on the agenda; failing this, businesses will be hamstrung and unable to compete in the international marketplace.

Government Incentives, Bane or Blessing?

In countries where liberalisation is being promoted as the road to economic salvation, the availability of financial incentives to producers is made out to be a bad thing. Lower tariff rates, duty free raw materials, and special interest rates fall into the category of financial incentives.

Where such incentives are provided by government, they are regarded as subsidies and are heavily criticised, especially by international lending agencies which maintain that subsidies encourage inefficiencies and allow producers to sell products at artificial rates. This, in their view, distorts true prices in a market economy.

This demand for a 'level playing field' which seeks to ensure that no player has an unfair advantage does not take into account the fact that there are numerous subsidies which remain in place in developed countries, particularly in the area of agriculture. As long as this is the situation there can be no fairness in the competition for markets in these countries. It is the task of governments in developing countries to negotiate a more equitable arrangement in this regard.

Although there are questions related to financial incentives there are other types of assistance which are available to business operators. Each entrepreneur should seek to determine what technical assistance programmes are available, what are the relevant training opportunities, as well as opportunities for joint-ventures and partnerships.

Formal versus Informal Operators

In any economy the size of the informal sector is of interest to government. In Latin America and the Caribbean the informal sector has grown at a rapid rate and has attracted large sums of money in micro-enterprise assistance programmes. The concern of governments, traditionally, has been how to bring this sector into the formal economy as they utilise governments' scarce resources – for example, in health and education – without making any appreciable contribution to government revenue.

Informal operators resist enrolment in the formal sector for a number of reasons, mainly the high cost of formal registration and the fact that this opens them to direct taxation. Companies which are formally registered also have to fulfill complex reporting requirements.

It is for governments to create the incentive framework which will make it attractive for micro-enterprise and informal small business operators to see the advantage in being part of the formal system. It must be noted, however, that where the legal framework is adequate – as in Jamaica – it is difficult for small business to escape formal registration.

Know the Rules

The rules and regulations which apply to various aspects of doing business are many. Every entrepreneur should take the time to procure, read, and understand brochures and pamphlets related to the government agencies with which he must deal. He should know the regulations governing:

- the import and export of goods (raw materials,motor vehicles, business supplies, what is on restricted lists, what is the rate of duty);
- the purchase of machinery and equipment (specifications as to size, capacity, emissions, power requirements);
- various licences and certificates which have to be obtained. These may be for the business, (for example a spirit licence for a liquor store), or professional and health licences;

- zoning of industrial activity;
- various legal reporting requirements.

Excessive bureaucracy is one of the hazards of entrepreneurship. Unfortunately, government red tape is a fact of life and your best bet is to have a full knowledge of the systems within which you have to operate. Developing sound personal alliances is a useful strategy; having the right contacts can save you time and money.

Entrepreneurial Responsibility

The entrepreneurial society can fall victim to wanton self-interest if there is no guiding force. A private sector which is the engine of growth may be regarded as the ultimate triumph of democracy, but we must not forget that the private sector, by its very nature is guided by self-interest.

Governments must see that part of their role is to guide the efforts of individuals toward the common good, which in the end will afford a measure of equity in the spread of resources and opportunities. This will ultimately make for a better life for all.

Where there is a common agenda for development and where government and private individuals hold to similar ideals, where government is your friend and not your enemy, when policies encourage your efforts, the spirit of entrepreneurship flourishes.

16 ENTREPRENEURSHIP AND THE NEW ENVIRONMENTAL ORDER

Time is Running Out

The Green Revolution is here. Whether we like it or not, the world is moving passionately towards that point where concerns for the protection of the physical environment will be foremost on the agenda for economic growth and social change. Sir Shridath Ramphal in his book *Our Country, The Planet* concludes:

> The war for human survival is unlike other wars. It is not a matter of winners and losers. Each must lose that all may win. Only to the extent that individual nations accept limits and thresholds can there be collective victory. It is not a war of man against man, nation against nation, but rather a war of humanity against unsustainable living. It is the only war we can afford. Only through enlightened change can humanity hope to triumph.

Matters of environmental conservation concern every inhabitant of this planet and time is running out for *homo sapiens*. He has fouled his nest and must take urgent action to repair the damage where possible and guard against future abuse.

Industrial Development the Culprit?

Action for environmental conservation is intricately linked with economic activity, and this factor has proven to be the greatest deterrent to the progress of programmes for conservation. The airline industry, for example, is perhaps one of the greatest pollutants of the atmosphere. The emissions of flourocarbons from jet aircraft have the potential to destroy the vital ozone layer at a rapid rate. Who would dare to introduce another constraint into the agenda of that already troubled industry? Yet it must be done; our survival depends upon it.

Many large manufacturing corporations which operate internationally, have experienced from time to time the wrath of consumers and persons who reside within a radius affected by toxic emissions, unfortunate accidents or the disposal of hazardous waste. We have yet to fully compute the damage caused by the Chernobyl disaster or the oil spill of the tanker *Exxon Valdes*. Insurance claims against super tanker spills have served to change the face of the re-insurance industry. Union Carbide in India, Nestlé in South Africa, bauxite companies in Jamaica all had their negative experiences with public perception of the effect that their activities have had upon the human and physical environment.

Progressive companies now seek to develop the kind of public relations and promotional programmes which present their corporate image as one conscious of environmental constraints and willing to spearhead and support environmental action. These so-called 'green companies' are far-sighted in their positioning in preparation for the tightening of environmental regulations.

Conservation versus Development

The dialogue on conservation versus development has gathered momentum. Are they compatible? The concept of sustainable development seeks to juxtapose the various components of development with imperatives for environmental and social sustainability in such a way as to provide a workable formula to future activity.

While the greatest abusers of the natural environment have been the industrialised countries, there is increasing concern about the role of poverty in environmental degradation. Growing populations in Africa and Asia are caught in the natural fallout of climatic shifts. Excessive rainfall on the one hand and desertification on the other, threaten the economic base of many countries.

International assistance agencies, in response to these

challenges, have sought to design loan and grant programmes in such a way as to force developing countries to make a committment to environmental conservation. They have met with some resistance, however, as cash starved nations do not have the wherewithal to mount costly environmental conservation programmes, many of which will necessitate change in the way the populace has been earning its livelihood for centuries.

The Enterprise for the Americas Initiative, the brainchild of George Bush, linked debt reduction with environmental conservation. Jamaica has been a model in the promotion of this strategy, where debt repayment made in Jamaican dollars goes into an environmental fund to be used mainly by non-government organisations in community-based environmental and child survival programmes.

Agenda 21, as presented at the Rio Conference of 1992 proposes actions which will have serious implications for the way business is done. The USA was hesitant in signing the conventions dealing with bio-diversity and clean air for that very reason. The financial implications for industries which must re-tool and perhaps change systems of production, introduce new technologies, finance research and develop new methods of treating hazardous waste are great. Many businesses would face closure with the introduction of such stringent regulations.

Tighter Regulations

Despite the cost, the world movement is towards a tighter regulatory framework for manufacturing and extractive industries. Such considerations transcend national boundaries and have implications for trading relationships.

A number of international conventions exist, for example CITES which seeks to inhibit trading involving protected species. Elephant and rhinoceros tusks, green turtle shells and crocodile skins all fall under this agreement.

In other cases, exporting countries have to conform to the environmental and health regulations of the countries whose markets they wish to access. This has serious cost implications for the way the Third World does business.

The motor vehicle industry will be subject to tighter controls as the number of vehicles grows and places serious pressure on fuel use and air quality. The role of timber as a raw material for mass production of paper and wood products will also be in question. The destruction of tropical forests is already receiving serious attention. Jamaica, for example, reportedly has the highest rate of deforestation in the world. And, hundreds of thousands of square miles of tropical forest in the Amazon Basin are being destroyed annually to make way for cattle, crops and other commercial activity.

The matter of non-biodegradable waste products is one of serious concern. Research is now turning attention to the use of recycled material. This will have effects on the extractive industries which may face reduced demand and find that they will have to cease operations altogether to accommodate the shift in technology.

The bauxite industry has already experienced a reduction in sales due partly to the use of the recycled metal, aluminium. Japanese researchers have announced success in creating totally synthetic material with interesting features of flexibility and durability. The world of the twenty-first century may require for its consumption needs little that has a natural base in the traditional sense.

What Can this Planet Support?

The basic tenet of environmental conservation is, in effect, a sustainable lifestyle. What can this planet support? The greatest deterrent to sound environmental practices is wanton consumerism on the part of developed societies, and ignorance and poverty on the part of the majority of the world's population in developing countries. Environmental conservation programmes will only succeed when they embrace the total needs of mankind and seek to engender some equity in the use of the Earth's resources.

New Entrepreneurial Opportunities

You may ask, "What has all this got to do with entrepreneurship?" The new environmental agenda, while having serious implications for the survival of many industries, nevertheless presents untold opportunities for the entrepreneurial minded.

New horizons for research will be opened. Products based on natural ingredients, for example fertilisers and insecticides, will seize the market. New strategies for recycling and using recycled material will find ready investors. In fact, one company in California is already utilising recycled plastic soda bottles to manufacture fabric.

Farmers who develop natural methods of farming and who process and market their products as being environmentally friendly, are beginning to has pride of place in the market of a generation who has a growing consciousness of health issues.

Eco-tourism is a promising area, as the green revolution spreads into the consciousness of a generation battered by ethnic and civil strife and persistent economic recession. Countries which do not show that they have some respect for their physical environment and which do not take measures to deal with sewage treatment and waste disposal, the preservation of natural landscapes and bio-diversity, will not find themselves high on the visiting list of the tourist of tomorrow.

Opportunities abound for the provision of health foods, herbal remedies, natural based drugs and personal fitness programmes. The preoccupation with healthy lifestyles is all part of the new 'green mix'.

These are all areas of challenge to the entrepreneur: how to create wealth from the shifting paradigm, how to develop products and attract investments which will make them earn their keep in the marketplace.

If you are already in business you would do well to inform yourself of what environmental regulations now apply to your business and which are likely to apply in the future. The type of raw materials which you use should be considered. Is the main input renewable or non-renewable. Is it likely to be affected by environmental regulations now or later? What about your product? What is likely to be its lifespan in the marketplace of increasingly sophisticated and informed users?

The following summarises the key questions for

consideration as you seek to bring your enterprise in line with standard environmental regulations:

- **What is the nature of your primary raw material.** Is it renewable or non-renewable? Are there likely to be difficulties in securing it in the short term?

- **The environmental safety of other raw materials** which form part of your production process. Cleaning fluids, solvents, catalysts, fertilisers, pesticides, products which yield residual potentially poisonous minerals such as mercury, lead, arsenic etc.

- **Safety procedures in your production process.** Are workers protected from toxic substances? Are such substances stored and used in line with regulations? How are they disposed of?

- Do you make adequate **provision for the use or disposal of by-products?** Useful by-products could spawn lucrative satellite enterprises.

- **Waste disposal** is an area of critical concern. Is your method of disposal in keeping with sound environmental practices, bearing in mind potential harmful pollution of air and water?

- **Is your packaging environmentally friendly?** Or will the plastic bags and bottles that invade our beaches be part of your doing? Does your packaging give accurate information on the contents of your product?

- If you are in the service industry, **is your market likely to survive the environmental conditionalities** with which all growing economies will be forced to comply? If not your market may soon be extinct.

Sound environmental practices in your business might be tedious but they are nonetheless necessary. They will protect your business in the future and save you the human cost in the event of some mishap – an occurence not restricted to big business alone.

CASE IN POINT

Arnold was a small business operator serving a well identified niche market through the manufacture of lead carbon batteries. Taxi and haulage operators found his cheaper prices attractive. Unfortunately, not enough attention was paid to the use of protective gear and the disposal of waste material. Arnold succumbed to lead poisoning and the business was closed by the health authorities. This is a sad story, but one which highlights the harmful consequences of ignoring environmental considerations when doing business.

In the final analysis, the opportunities created by this green revolution will outweigh the losses encountered in this period of transition. They can only result in a better life for all. The smart entrepreneur will look to these opportunities.

17 UTILISING YOUR SUPPORT SYSTEMS

There is Help Out There

The entrepreneur's road to success does not have to be a lonely one. There are agencies, programmes, data bases and a plethora of other opportunities which, if properly utilised, can make a difference to the efficiency and success of your enterprise.

The willingness to seek advice and to weigh alternatives will help you to avoid costly and frustrating mistakes. Although determination and self-confidence are important qualities for success, being willing to work with others is also important, particularly when seeking the information you need.

Information

The key word which must always be in your head is 'information'. Make a habit of informing yourself. **Do not operate on assumptions**. In cases where you must do so, at least ensure that they are informed assumptions. Many of you may remember the saying: 'Assume makes an ass of you and me.'

One of your key interests, no matter what your entrepreneurial enterprise might be, is the state of the related technology and innovation. There are certain questions which you should be asking yourself continuously:

- What new innovations and technology have come on stream?
- Is my machinery or equipment obsolete?
- Is there any current research in my field?
- What are the new market trends? Export opportunities?
- Who are the new players in the field? How well are they doing?

- What new opportunities has my business created?
- How can I improve my service?
- What training opportunities are there for myself and my staff?

Investment promotion and business development agencies normally carry data bases which will allow you to determine state of the art information in your area of interest. It is better to utilise information from periodicals and bulletins than from lengthy texts or bulky reports which may be dated. It is wise to subscribe to journals related to your field; for example, it is near impossible to keep abreast of movements in the computer industry without access to a range of periodicals.

Participation

It is also advisable to become a member of any related association or interest group which may serve a useful lobby function in securing benefits for your industry, or the industry which you serve. For example, in the field of tourism all related businesses have a responsibility to be part of the decision-making process. In economies which are vulnerable to policy change this type of participation is vital for stability.

You will find that the shared experience with operators of similar enterprises will enhance your ability to manage your own operations and avoid needless errors.

Partnerships and Business Networking

Such an outward looking philosophy will also present greater opportunities for business alliances and partnerships for production. You may wish to joint-bid on a large contract with a sister enterprise, thus expanding your production capacity. There are also opportunities to purchase raw materials in bulk at reduced prices through joint buying.

Many entrepreneurs shy away from any type of joint activity, preferring to hide behind suspicion and ignorance because they do not possess the negotiating skills. **Training in the art of negotiation is vital for you.** It will promote not only your sales capability but your ability to position and to benefit from new technologies of cooperation.

Partnerships, then, do not only serve for business ownership, but in support services and backward linkages as well. For example, many craft manufacturers operate through a network of partnerships.

CASE IN POINT
Beulah operates a successful craft enterprise. She designs and manufactures straw goods mainly for the tourist market. Over the years she has developed a cadre of satellite cottage industries with people engaged in the planting, reaping and plaiting of straw and the manufacture of certain product lines for which they have been properly trained. Employing mainly women, she has found this to be the most advantageous means of operating. It reduces her overhead costs and gives them a flexible time schedule.

Such types of partnerships will be utilised more in the future as problems associated with urban life will drive increasing numbers of people to the suburbs, only to have commuting hampered by congestion on the highways. Fortunately, new facilities for telecommuting will make it unnecessary for large numbers of persons to be physically present in the workplace. You will find that more and more the orientation will be to monitor productivity rather than to supervise bodies.

Another strategy which you would do well to explore is the development of sub-contracting relationships. Take for example, a large furniture enterprise which operates retail outlets only, and sub-contracts orders to a number of small manufacturers who agree upon volume to be supplied, as well as design and quality.

The symbiotic nature of such a relationship can extend to the provision of venture capital investments, technology transfers and a range of other benefits. It is important to note that the initiative does not have to come from the so-called 'mother' industry, but a group of potential 'sub-contractees' can come together and approach a large company. In fact, in this way they are able to negotiate more favourable contractual terms.

Training

Entrepreneurs, particularly in the small business sector are not as vigilant as they should be in the use of training facilities. The interest tends to die once the business is up and running. This is a mistake. Very often the solutions to the very problems which keep you away from training interventions would be found through your participation. Entrepreneurs are prime candidates for what I call 'woods for the trees syndrome', their absorbtion with the details of daily crises have robbed them of the ability to see the big picture.

The right amount of participation in related training sessions, seminars and workshops will enable you and your employees to keep the big picture in focus while equipping you to better fight the fires which occur on a daily basis.

Training is not only relevant for you, but for your employees as well. Human Resource Development is not the purview of large companies only. No matter how small the enterprise, the people deserve to be as efficient as they can be. Encourage employees to be on the look-out for relevant training programmes, and to continuously seek to upgrade their skills. The cost to you will show adequate returns in due time.

Business Counselling and Consultancy

The numerous technical assistance programmes promoted by both the public and private sector, provide business counselling and consultancy interventions at minimal cost to you, or sometimes at no cost at all. Many entrepreneurs hesitate to use such services, regarding the officers involved as neophytes who know nothing about business. "If they know so much, why aren't they running their own businesses?" is the question often asked. The answer is that they prefer to be business counsellors, and they *do* know something about business. They generally have the breadth of experience and the specialised skills necessary for an in-depth analysis of your business problems.

For you to invite the services of a business counsellor you have to acknowledge that there is a business problem and be prepared to get assistance. You have to be willing to invest time and money in the upgrading of your business. Even if things are going well, it may be that they could be better. Bringing a business counsellor in could be similar to getting a medical check-up, just to see that everything is alright.

A business consultant is usually called in when there is a specific problem of sufficient importance to warrant specialised treatment. It could be in preparation for venture capital investment for example, or preceding a public offer of shares, some shift in production technology, or major expansion.

The beneficial effects of these interventions will never be seen, however, if you do not make use of the action plan agreed upon. The strategic direction identified should be taken seriously by you as you seek to avoid unnecessary hazards of entrepreneurship.

18 THE CHALLENGE OF THE FUTURE

World Trends

We are living in exciting times, as we stand on the threshold of the 21st century. We face not only the close of a century but the beginning of a new millennium. The trend of world events driven by new innovations and technology, is moving humanity inexorably towards this new dawn. It is as if mankind is being drawn into this vortex of unimaginable possibilities with frightening rapidity.

What is certain is the uncertainty of the future. We cannot help but echo the sentiments of the French poet Jean Valery when he said: "The future isn't what it used to be."

For the last decade of the twentieth century we have seen momentous change in political systems with the end of the Cold War and the dismantling of communism; a united Germany and the Berlin wall reduced to material for souvenirs, the Israeli and the PLO engaged in a historic peace accord.

In the field of technology there is the increasing sophistication of the micro-chip, genetic engineering, the search for a cure for AIDS while in the economic sphere the new power of trading blocs and individual interest groups all converge into this mix of what we call the future.

The Power of the Individual

Yet in all of this we stand as individuals – man and woman, even more conscious of our potential, being made more powerful by these very innovations; man and woman with the entrepreneurial zeal which will lead to our self-actualisation being confident that we can face tomorrow.

What will tomorrow demand of us? What tomorrow

demands is not so much an offering of some material thing as the strength of the beliefs which we hold. It will not be so much through the acquisition of wealth to take us in the future as the ability to continue to acquire wealth. **Your success will be predicated upon your ability to remain relevant.**

You will be required to separate your individuality from the process of your business, to accept strangers, and venture far afield both in marketing and in technology. You will have to come to terms with automation and computer applications and the new dynamics between people and productivity. Mergers, acquisitions and buy-outs will remain very much a part of business, firms will either move with the processes of change or die.

You will have to cultivate a philosophy of tolerance of change and a flexibility which makes your own personal re-tooling a matter of course. Your intuitive skills will have to be honed in order to stand you in good stead as you use the searchlight of a practised eye to spot new entrepreneurial opportunities, and new relationships between people and events.

You will have to think systems rather than structure, and develop the tolerance which goes with the fluidity of response necessary for life as a constantly evolving process. You will need to possess the skills to redesign systems to meet the demand for new products and develop competence in meeting the needs of a market that will be increasingly informed and selective. The reality of the marketplace will take precedence over policies and economic strategies.

Peter Drucker, in his book *Managing for the Future* concludes that:

> ...the new reality means that we can no longer control the economic 'weather' of recession and boom cycles, unemployment savings and spending rates, but only the 'climate' – avoiding protectionism, or educating the working population to function in a knowledge society. In short, preventive medicine instead of blind attempts at short-term fixes.

The challenge of the future is to find the real solutions to persistent social, political and economic problems. The strong, the astute, the energetic, the creative, the intellectually competent will triumph. They will separate themselves from the chaff of indecision and wanton materialism and bring some sanity to bear on the momentum of events, because deep within them is the age-old imprint of the human soul that dictates that man must be master of his circumstances for, essentially, throughout time he remains the same:

> ...a generation goes, and a generation comes,
> But the earth remains for ever.
> What has been is what will be,
> And what has been done is what will be done;
> And there is nothing new under the sun...

Appendix

CURING THE ILLNESS: A CHECKLIST FOR ACTION

The hazards of entrepreneurship are ever present, but there are strategies for dealing with them. The trick is to inform yourself of the various possibilities and develop your own strategic plan based on your past experiences. You should then be able to deal with those things that are within your control, and have reserve energy to cope with those outside of it.

Businesses behave in many ways like organisms; if they are starved of life-giving cash they will die. It is equally injurious to them if they have no means of disposing of their products. They have to develop symbiotic relationships with other businesses in the same way that organisms depend upon one another. Their internal functioning depends upon the delicate balance between their component parts, and malfunction of one part can affect the whole.

So delicate and complex is the challenge of business management that the entrepreneur must equip himself with the skills to spot the symptoms of illness and to seek a cure. This summary of the more prevalent symptoms will help in trouble shooting and improve the manager's ability to avoid crises.

SYMPTOM	POSSIBLE CAUSE
Chronic shortage of working capital	Initial undercapitalisation, business not adequately financed to get off the ground
	Poor management of receivables
	Incorrect pricing due to improper computation of cost of sales
	No provision for contingencies
	Funds are being siphoned off for personal use, development of infrastructure, business expansion, etc.

SYMPTOM	POSSIBLE CAUSE
	Escalating costs due to instability of the macroeconomic environment
	Poor financial record-keeping
Noticeable reduction in sales	Change in quality of the product offered due to poor quality control
	Pricing no longer competitive
	Packaging unattractive and impractical
	A competitor making inroads into your market share
	A change in consumer taste
	Pressure on disposable income as a result of macroeconomic factors
	No informed marketing plan
	Promotions not in place, not reaching the targetted groups
	Changes in technology rendering your product obsolete.
Rapid staff turnover	Staff is dissatisfied with your management style
	Staff lack confidence in the strength of the business
	Staff not carefully selected, do not have the right skills and aptitudes

SYMPTOM	POSSIBLE CAUSE
	Job tasks and responsibilities not clearly outlined, leads to confusion and demotivation
	Poor pay with no opportunity for profit sharing
Unending series of crises	Poor planning
	Lack of experience in the factors of production
	Outmoded or inappropriate machinery/equipment
	Management systems not clearly defined
	Too few people to do too many things, increasing the risk of human error
Numerous customer complaints	Lack of regard for customer service as an art and a science
	No serious attention to quality control
	Lack of training in the delivery of quality service
	Production process tardy leading to delays in delivery
	No provision for legitimate feedback for customers

Glossary

Amortise — To reduce debt by regular payments over a specified period of time.

Balance sheet — A financial report which shows the company's assets, liabilities and owners' equity at a given date.

Break-even position — This is the point at which the company's sales equals the cost of producing these sales. Break-even analysis is used to determine the point at which the volume of sales will cover fixed and variable costs. If sales exceed the break-even point profits will be produced; if they are below the company will record losses.

Cash Flow — This usually refers to the amount of cash that is available to cover operating costs.The company's cash flow is related to its income and expenditure over a given period. Reliable cash flow projections are necessary for good money management.

Collateral — An asset pledged to a lender by the borrower, to be held against a loan until it is repaid. If the borrower fails to repay in the specified time the lender has the legal right to sell the collateral to pay off the loan.

Debt financing — Financing the business operations through loans and other types of debt.

Deficit — This occurs when liabilities and debts are more than the income and assets of a company. It can also refer to an excess of expenditure over budget.

Development finance — Money that is available through development banks and their affiliated lending institutions.

Equity	Funds invested by shareholders in a company.
Exit clause	Statement outlining the conditions under which an agreement or contract may be terminated.
Fixed costs	Costs that remain constant regardless of the sales volume, for example salaries, interest expense, rent and insurance costs.
Foreclose	When a bank takes the decision to terminate a loan and dispose of collateral held against outstanding amounts.
Gross domestic product	The total value of goods and services produced in a country over a specified period of time.
Liquidity	The ability of an individual or a company to convert assets into cash or cash equivalents without significant loss.
Macroeconomic	Relating to the country's economy as a whole, for example taking into consideration unemployment, inflation and monetary policy.
Marketing	The process by which goods and services are moved from the provider to the consumer.
Market niche	A particular segment of the market that is most likely to purchase the goods and services being produced.
Production capability	The volume of goods and services which a business can produce over a given time period.
Profit	The excess in income which remains after a business has met all its costs and has made the required provisions.

Promotions	The process by which the public is apprised of the goods and services produced by a company.
Quality control	The process of ensuring that products are produced at a consistent standard.
Receivables	Money owed to a business for goods or services purchased.
Seasonality	Variations in demand for goods or services produced due to climate, holidays, vacations etc.
Security	*See* Collateral
Turnover	The number of times that stock has to be replaced, for example one year.
Undercapitalisation	The situation in which a business does not have enough capital to carry on its operations.
Variable costs	Costs that change with the level of production, for example raw material or direct labour.
Venture capital	Type of financing which provides equity for a business or in the case of a loan where the lender is willing to share the risk.
Working capital	Cash available to finance the operations of a business.

Bibliography

Autry, James A. *Love and Profit: The Art of Caring Leadership*; (Avon Books, N.Y. 1991).

Drucker, Peter F. *Innovation and Entrepreneurship: Practice and Principles.* (Heinemann, London, 1985).

Drucker, Peter F. *Managing for Results.* (Heinemann Professional Publishing 1989).

Drucker, Peter F. *Managing for the Future.* (Butterworth, Heinemann,1992).

Gerber, Michael E. *The E Myth: Why Small Businesses Don't Work and What to do About it.* (Harper Business. A Division of Harper Collins Publishers, 1986).

Levitt, Theodore. *Marketing for Business Growth.* (McGraw-Hill, new York 1974).

Montagu, Ashley as quoted in Jongeward, Dorothy and Scott, Dru. *Women as Winners:Transactional Analysis for Personal Growth.* (Addison-Wesley Publishing Company, Mass., 1976).

Naisbett, John and Aburdene, Patricia. *Megatrends 2000: Ten New Directions for the l990s.* (Avon Books, New York,1990).

Ramphal, Shridath, Sir. *Our Country, the Planet: Forging a Partnership for Survival.* (Island Press,Washington D.C.,1992).

Rath, Sarah as quoted in Jongeward, Dorothy and Scott, Dru. *Women as Winners: Transactional Analysis for Personal Growth.* (Addison-Wesley Publishing Company, Mass.,1976).

Say, J.B. as cited in Drucker, Peter F. *Innovation and Entrepreneurship: Practice and Principles.* (Heinemann, London, 1985).

Schumacher, E.F. *Small is Beautiful: Economics as if People Mattered.* (Harper and Row Publishers, New York, 1975).

Schumpeter, Joseph as cited in Drucker, Peter F. *Innovation and Entrepreneurship: Practice and Principles.* (Heinemann, London, 1985).

www.ingramcontent.com/pod-product-compliance
Ingram Content Group UK Ltd.
Pitfield, Milton Keynes, MK11 3LW, UK
UKHW041824200726
13854UKWH00002BA/536

9 789768 184030